I,
Charlotte Forten,
BLACK and FREE

BY THE AUTHOR

I,
Charlotte Forten,
BLACK and FREE

~~~~~~

By Polly Longsworth

Thomas Y. Crowell Company   New York

MANUFACTURED IN THE UNITED STATES OF AMERICA
L.C. Card 79-109901
1   2   3   4   5   6   7   8   9   10

For Laura and Anne

Acknowledgments

I am deeply indebted to Ray Allen Billington's edition of Charlotte L. Forten's diary, entitled *A Free Negro in the Slave Era: The Journal of Charlotte L. Forten,* published in 1953 by the Dryden Press, Inc., and reissued in paperback as a Collier Book by the Crowell-Collier Publishing Company in 1961. I, CHARLOTTE FORTEN, BLACK AND FREE is based upon Billington's book and is as close a re-creation of Miss Forten's life and experiences as I am capable of achieving. The original diary is in the Moorland Collection of Howard University. My thanks are due to Professor John William Ward of Amherst College for reading my manuscript and to the reference librarians at the Robert Frost Library, Amherst College, who were endlessly helpful in tracing needed books. And I am very grateful to my editor, Matilda W. Welter, for introducing me to Charlotte Forten and for patiently and wisely guiding me throughout the writing of this book.

Polly Longsworth

Chapter 1

~·~·~·~·~·~·~·~·~·~·~·~·~·~·~·~·~·~·

I smile to think what a thin, shy wisp of a girl I was when I first arrived in Salem. Into a New England May I stepped in 1854, and found trees full-budded, birds in plenty, and soft warm breezes blowing in from the sparkling ocean across the aristocratic old town and its surrounding woods and farmlands.

I, too, felt full-budded, full of promise and yearning, and ready at sixteen for a new life. Full of hope is what I'm trying to say. It's what I brought with me from Philadelphia, all the way by railroad car (where I sat among the colored), by sailing ship from New York, then again by railroad. But the second time there was no colored car, and hope felt ratified.

Behind, in Philadelphia, I left everything I loved: my father, my aunts and uncles and cousins, my dear but motherless home, and my Uncle Robert's home in nearby Byberry. These had composed my familiar world until the journey to Salem.

Father and even Grandfather had talked of New England so often and in such glowing terms that I knew I would love it there as well. In Massachusetts, the birthplace of the nation's freedom, lay more promise than in any other state of the Union that people of our race might live without persecution. In going there, I cherished, too, the secret wish that Father would soon join me, and that we would establish near Boston a home for future generations of Fortens. It was my dream.

I had been educated at home, for Philadelphia schools were segregated. Father refused to support the galling system and instead engaged tutors or called upon my aunts to instruct me in arithmetic and grammar, in history, Latin, and French, in music and the natural sciences. My own love of books and desire to improve my mind led me down other paths as well.

To be educated at home is a lonely process, and perhaps the sense that this was so prompted Father to make arrangements with his friends, the Remonds, in Salem for me to live with them. The Salem public schools had been desegregated for a decade, and it was planned that I should attend the Higginson Grammar School there for a year or more with other girls my age.

To Salem, lovely Salem, I went then that poignant spring, leaving with few regrets the already suffocatingly hot City of Brotherly Love, home of Independence, where I was not allowed to enter theater or museum or ice-cream parlor, where my taxpaying father could not vote, where liberty is guaranteed for those whose skin is white and justice for all is a mockery. I left, I thought, for the "Cradle of Liberty," but I had not been at Boston a fortnight when it was demonstrated to all the world that that city, too, was ruled by prejudice.

The Remond home in Salem, which I then entered for the first time, was a modest but comfortable dwelling situated at 9 Dean Street, adjacent to the principal street in Salem. Master of the household was Charles Lennox Remond, whose fame as lecturer for the Massachusetts Anti-Slavery Society had spread far, even across the ocean to fair England. A small, wiry man, intelligent and genteel in appearance, he seemed genuinely pleased to welcome me into his family. Indeed, he had many times been so welcomed into the Forten home in Philadelphia, but never for such an extended period as I was about to spend under his roof. Of Mr. Remond, I shall tell more later. Suffice to say now that he had earned two informal titles which frequently came to my ears. His spare neatness, faultless dress, and skill as a horseman had earned him the appellation, "the Count D'Orsay of the Anti-Slavery Movement." I also heard him called "the colored Wendell Phillips," in reference to his eloquence upon the platform.

It was Mrs. Remond to whom I became instantly attached. Her glad cry of "Charlotte, dear, how happy we are to have you" was joyous greeting to the very weary young lady climbing from a carriage before her door. When I add that Amy Matilda Remond was childless, as I was motherless, you will perhaps surmise the bond of affection that quickly grew between us.

She had arranged for me the pleasantest of rooms at the top of her house, with a comfortable bed and a desk, washstand, wardrobe, and great braided rag rug. The window provided intimacy with the treetops and the birds, and brought to my nostrils the smells of salt water and the wharf.

Sharing the home was Mr. Remond's brother, who operated a hairdressing establishment on Washington Street, and his sister, Sarah, nearing forty years of age, who frequently traveled and lectured with her brother for the Anti-Slavery Society.

Perhaps now I had better introduce myself. I am Charlotte Forten. I am a person of color, but have never been a slave. Nor was my father, nor my grandfather, nor any of *his* family as far as he could trace, a slave. At the time of which I write, we were free Negroes among nearly five hundred thousand free persons of color in this country, and yet while free, we were victims of the cruelest hatred and tyranny and the most absurd prejudice originating in that Southern curse, slavery. If at times my burden depressed me, it was because all my life I had known slights and insults; if at times I could rejoice, it was because there were in the land persons convinced of the moral wrong of slavery, and occasionally they were heard.

To describe New England, and most particularly Boston and its environs as it seemed to my fresh eyes that spring of 1854, I must recapture its very special atmosphere, for I sensed currents of excitement that could not be explained entirely by the quickened climate. There was an energy abroad among New Englanders that I had not known at home. It was shortly revealed as a moral energy, a shining forth of conscience that charged the very air one breathed.

New England has always had an identifiable conscience, and perhaps always will. It was instilled in the region in such concentrated form by the Puritans who founded the Massachusetts Bay Colony that its quality may never be diluted. While it is not always in evidence, when stimulated by recognizable evil New England's conscience reveals its intrinsic strength.

New England had been most recently aroused by the Fugitive Slave Act, which was one section of the Compromise of 1850. North and South had been quarreling for some time over the vast new lands that were opening up in the Mid and Far West. The Southern economic system was based upon Negro labor, and Southerners wanted to take slaves with them to settle the new territories. Northerners objected. Northern industrialists and businessmen tolerated Southern slavery in order to carry on business, but were not interested in seeing slavery extended into the West. They wanted it limited to the states where it already existed. A few Northerners wanted to abolish slavery everywhere. Most were concerned only with the new soil, which they were determined should be free.

With the Compromise of 1850, North and South finally reached an agreement about the new territories, admitting California as a free state and leaving the decision about slavery up to the new settlers of the Utah and New Mexico tracts. The compromise also abolished slave trading in the nation's capital (although that sickening performance merely retreated across the Potomac River into Virginia). But the section of it that immediately became a burr under the saddle and a powerful stimulus to Northern consciences was the fugitive slave clause.

The Fugitive Slave Law gave Southern slaveholders the right to pursue runaway slaves into the free states of the North, to capture the miserable creatures and take them back into slavery. This was not the first fugitive law. There had been earlier ones, despite Northern feeling that states' rights were being violated. But the 1850 bill was the strongest fugitive ruling yet imposed. Federal marshals were charged with executing the law, and severe penalties awaited anyone assisting runaways.

Southern slaveowners at last had the federal guarantees they needed to track down slaves who escaped, and great numbers of them set about slave hunting with vengeance. Incidents occurred in Pennsylvania, in New York, in Ohio, in Massachusetts. For the many Negro fugitives living in the North, there was little choice after 1850 but to go into hiding or escape to Canada. Hundreds did the latter, and the underground railroad was strengthened to assist them. Vigilance committees of white citizens formed in the cities to patrol streets and hotels, and be on the lookout for Southern agents. Free Negroes lived from 1850 on

with the ever-present knowledge that there was little
to prevent our being kidnapped into slavery as effectively as any fugitive. It had happened enough times to
plant a small but abiding fear within. As long as slavery existed, no colored person ever would be free.

By the time I went to Salem, resentment at being
victim to a despised system of social justice had spread
widely in the North. The resentment was perceptible
in Philadelphia, but near Boston one sensed a mood of
righteous defiance. Several incidents testing the Fugitive Slave Law had provoked Bostonians to great
heights of moral indignation.

Through the newspapers I had been aware of the
thundering proclamations of Theodore Parker, minister of the largest Unitarian congregation in the city
and "minister at large" to all fugitive slaves. Superior
to man-made laws, preached Parker, was the higher
law of truth established by God. When man-made laws
did not suffice, allegiance to higher law was justified.
"I call upon all men who love law," he cried, "to vio-
late and break the Fugitive Slave Bill; to do it peace-
ably if they can, forcibly if they must." Not everyone
agreed with Parker, but many prominent voices took
up the cry, and many were persuaded to resist the laws
protecting slavery. Two instances met with success.
The fugitive couple Ellen and William Craft were
helped by Parker and the Boston Vigilance Committee
to escape to Europe. One Frederick Wilkins, called
Shadrach, was daringly rescued in broad daylight from
the Boston Court House by a mob of blacks and whites,
some of whom were later brought to trial but never

8 I, CHARLOTTE FORTEN, BLACK AND FREE

convicted. In a more recent case, however—that of young Seth Nims—the South had triumphed, and the Fugitive Law was effectively carried out.

All these events I knew about, for our home in Philadelphia was a gathering place for people involved in the antislavery cause. I found life in Salem quite similar. Here, as there, conversation at the dinner table and in the parlor turned on abolition. Our guests were abolitionists and people sympathetic to the cause. The newspapers we read were the *Liberator* and the *National Anti-Slavery Standard*. The lectures we attended promoted emancipation.

Brought up in the midst of these affairs, I could never for a moment forget that three million of my race lived in bondage. My most intense yearning since childhood had been to serve the cause that sought to end slavery. But what I, as a Negro, and a woman besides, might do to help my fellow man was far from clear. Yet I was determined to be prepared when some avenue of opportunity opened, and to this end worked furiously to educate myself.

As it happened, the process of getting an education was a particularly pleasant aspect of my Salem life. I enjoyed attending public school, and found association with so many girls my age very agreeable. They seemed to accept the presence of my darker skin calmly. I was received with smiles and courtesy, perhaps because the principal, Miss Mary Shepard, introduced me so warmly and so graciously. My outward reserve and awkwardness, both of which I possessed in good measure, disguised the keen fires of ambition seething within. Desiring more than just dwelling in harmony among my new classmates, I was fiercely determined to excel them in all my studies, to prove myself capable of high intellectual accomplishments, both for the sake of the cause to which I was devoted and to counter the assumption, met everywhere, that darker skin is evidence of biological inferiority.

Those first mornings I rose with the sun and birds, and was at my lessons before five o'clock. Waking early was a habit of my father's which I admired and with some effort imitated, so as to put every moment to good use. I sometimes felt quite frantic to hold back time while I read and learned, and would goad my laggard brain and feet each dawn, until one carried the other to my desk to work until breakfast.

Any feeling of strangeness in my new home was short-lived. Mrs. Remond knew how to soothe the kinks of adjustment, how to ease homesickness, and how to make me feel of service in her household. Besides, an event promptly occurred that took my mind off myself.

Two or three evenings after my arrival Mrs. Remond and Sarah and I were occupied quietly in the parlor while Mr. Remond and his brother attended a meeting of the Salem Anti-Slavery Society. At the request of those two ladies, who neither played nor sang, I sat at the piano attempting to do honor to the genius of Beethoven. They meanwhile sewed and listened attentively in chairs drawn near the west window to catch the last daylight. Mr. Remond's arrival home need not have interrupted my playing, but from the look on his face as he appeared in the parlor doorway, he obviously brought news.

"They've caught another fugitive," he announced as my fingers halted on the keys. "A fellow named Burns."

"Where?" "When?" "Who is he?"

The three questions, launched simultaneously, were warded off by Charles Remond's raised hands. "Last evening about teatime," he informed us. "Mr. Garrison wrote from Boston this morning, knowing we were meeting tonight. He gives details of the arrest and says there's to be a mass meeting at Faneuil Hall tomorrow night."

"Who is he, Charles?" Mrs. Remond repeated her question.

"Well, he's a slave who made his way up here from Virginia about two months ago. Anthony Burns is his name. He has been working in a clothing store on Brattle Street, but his former owner—a man named Colonel Suttle from Alexandria—traced him. Suttle came to Boston yesterday and had Marshal Butman arrest Burns and take him to the Court House. The poor fellow spent last night there under guard, and Commissioner Loring examined him for a while this morning. Richard Dana appeared first thing and offered to represent Burns, so he's fortunate there. Dana also managed a few days' delay in the proceedings to get his case ready. The trial is set for Monday now, which gives us just three days for action."

"Us?" queried Mrs. Remond.

"I mean anyone who's determined Burns isn't going

back into slavery, and that includes us," Charles Remond stated firmly, striking his fist on his well-tailored knee.

Sarah Remond rose to light a lamp beside the chair her brother had settled into. "He's assured a fair trial with Richard Dana's counsel, and I agree, he's fortunate to have it. There's probably not another lawyer in Boston, radical or Whig, who would defend a fugitive in court these days."

I, too, felt somewhat easier at heart for knowing that Richard Henry Dana would argue the fugitive's case. His was a name sweet to the ears of anyone anxious that personal liberties be extended to black men as well as white. Since the passage of the Fugitive Slave Law, Dana had stood with those who defied the right of Southerners to reach into the free states of the North to retrieve their runaway "property." Dana thought the Fugitive Law unconstitutional. "Law or no law," he had argued in 1850, "not a slave should be taken back from Massachusetts." Yet he also believed consistently in peaceful legal procedure, and in a time of passion, when strong feelings and even violence were rife, Dana's cool and sober disposition set him apart from those who would abandon legal means to achieve their purpose. If the Fugitive Slave Act was the law of the land, Dana would conduct the most powerful defense he could construct to combat it. No fugitive would be rendered to slavery for want of his greatest legal effort. But he was not ready to give way to theories on higher law.

"Excitement must be running high in Boston," said

Sarah. "What does Mr. Garrison say of the members of the Vigilance Committee?"

"Nothing of them, but they can't be sitting by," Mr. Remond replied. "The city is in quite a state, it seems. The police force has been doubled, and the militia stands ready. Sounds like the Sims affair all over again."

"No!" burst from my lips so explosively that the Remonds all turned sharply toward me. My indignation, aroused by the plight of this poor man who had done nothing but escape a bondage intolerably and wrongly imposed, and who was the unfortunate victim of one more contest between North and South, poured forth.

"No! It shan't be another Nims case! What has Burns done to be arrested like a criminal in the streets of Boston? Isn't he a man, created in God's image, living in a state where Negroes are free? How can people here allow slaveowners to pursue their evil ends in a free city? And why should the rights of evildoers be supported by law and the rights of the innocent and oppressed not exist?"

A wry smile appeared on Mr. Remond's face. "Charlotte, Charlotte," he calmed me in a firm, dispassionate voice. "I believe we shall see you upon the antislavery platform before long. It sounds to me as if there's a lot of your grandfather in you."

I blushed and glanced shyly at Sarah Remond to see how she with her experience as an orator for the Anti-Slavery Society was receiving news of a rival. But she was more interested in Anthony Burns than in me.

"What hope is there that he won't be taken back South?" Sarah asked her brother.

"I know only what is in Mr. Garrison's letter. He says public opinion is strongly with Burns. The passage of the Kansas-Nebraska Bill the other day was the final straw, and even men who supported the compromise four years ago are talking treason now."

Treason! It was a strong word, and a thrilling one. Yet it had been heard in Boston before in times of duress. As if I expected to hear treason advocated on every street corner, I was suddenly eager to go into the city myself to be part of whatever might occur.

"Perhaps there will be an attempt at rescue," suggested Mrs. Remond. "It worked with Shadrach, you remember."

"That was before such precautions as heavy police guards and chains around the Court House," replied Charles Remond. "Yet I'll guarantee the Vigilance Committee isn't unemployed tonight. Garrison says Dana intends to build his case around identity. There seems to be some chance Suttle can't prove this man is his fugitive. I suppose we'll learn more of that from the newspapers tomorrow."

"Some chance! That's hard to believe," Sarah objected. "What chance has a poor colored slave in the hands of men like Loring with his federal commission to administer the Fugitive Slave Law and a large fee to make sure he cooperates with the slavecatchers? He'll do all he can to send Burns south, and so will the United States marshal and the city marshal with the help of their deputies, and so will Mayor Smith with police and artillery to do his bidding!"

I knew that some of Sarah's bitterness stemmed from an incident of a year earlier. She had been rudely expelled from the New York Atheneum when visiting in that city, and while she had carried her complaint to the police court and eventually obtained an opinion sustaining the rights of colored persons, it had been a difficult battle, and the memory still rankled.

"Don't forget there's to be a meeting at Faneuil Hall tomorrow night," countered her brother. "That ought to be quite a demonstration of the people's feelings. Loring will have Wendell Phillips and Theodore Parker to contend with, and I shouldn't wonder if Colonel Suttle came off second best after that."

Charles Remond's attitude was optimistic enough that I went to bed that night hopeful and prayerful that Boston would not again send a colored man back to bondage, not again as the boy Seth Nims had been sent three years before in the dead of night, with three hundred soldiers and policemen for escort, back south to prison, to an almost fatal beating and the slave block.

The days that followed possessed a special validity for me, as momentous events occasionally do when coupled with some phenomenon of nature or physical experience, so that mind *and* senses respond to the event and record it indelibly upon the memory. It happened that the week of the Anthony Burns trial was one of vacation from school, a vacation which my classmates at Higginson Grammar School had eagerly anticipated, but which I, having so recently entered the school, felt slightly uneasy about, as if I had not properly earned the free time.

It was a week, too, of unusually luxurious spring weather, day after day dawning bright and balmy, filled with the soft fragrances of new blossoms, filled with the tender sights of infant leaves, of thrusting peonies, their burgeoning crown jewels held high, filled always with the loud song and twitterings of birds.

All this coincided with the annual meetings of the New England Anti-Slavery Society, which went on for three days at Melodeon Hall in Boston and provided me the opportunity I needed to go into the city to see for myself the general excitement there. Added to everything, Father was coming, according to prearranged plan, to attend the antislavery meetings as part of the delegation from Philadelphia. Although I had parted from him but ten days before, it seemed a lifetime in terms of new experiences and sensations, and I was overjoyed to see something as familiar and beloved as his handsome face in my new world.

Mr. Remond drove me to the depot to meet him on Saturday afternoon. Father had come almost directly to Salem, stopping at Boston between trains just long enough to learn the latest news.

"I should have come a day sooner, Charlotte," were his first words as we embraced beside the great hissing steam engine. "I missed some great doings in Boston last night."

"Hello, Robert," said Charles Remond, stretching

forth his hand. "You come at an eventful time. I take it the Faneuil Hall meeting was a good one."

"The largest crowd the building's ever had, they say, Charles. How are you?" Father's arm left my shoulders for a moment to fall upon Mr. Remond's. "Faneuil was packed to the doors, with the galleries and aisles filled and hundreds trying to get in."

Father proceeded then to tell us of the angry temper of the crowd, how Theodore Parker had brought it shouting to its feet by addressing his audience as "fellow subjects of Virginia," how Parker and Wendell Phillips, the most eloquent speaker the reform movement possessed, brought the people to a pitch of excitement by calling for their support of higher law, "The law of the people when they are sure they are right and determined to go ahead." Suddenly word was shouted from the back of the building that a mob was storming the Court House with the intent of rescuing Burns. People jumped from their seats and tried to rush to the Court House, but the jammed condition of the hall prevented quick exodus.

There was indeed a plot to free Burns. It had been set afoot by members of the Vigilance Committee, in particular a Worcester minister named Thomas Wentworth Higginson and a Negro abolitionist named Lewis Hayden. But lack of careful communication among the plot's leaders and the inability of necessary reinforcements to get out of Faneuil Hall in time to aid in storming the Court House caused it to fail. Higginson, Hayden, and a few others broke down the Court House door, but were beaten back by the many guards inside. In the scuffle one of the marshal's deputies was killed.

By the time Father finished this quick sketch of events, my eyes were shining both with admiration for the bravery of the rescuers and with tears for the failure of their attempt. "If so many are for Burns, then surely he'll go free," I said emphatically, looking at Father for his assurance. My father had assisted slaves escaping from the South through Philadelphia, and he was acquainted with the risks and terrors faced by runaways. In addition, he knew firsthand the forces with which anyone assisting fugitives had to deal: the Southerners who considered slaves their chattel; the commissioners and marshals and deputies, whose duty it was to uphold law; the unsympathetic Northerners who despised colored people or who, at best, just didn't want the problems caused by a growing population of free Negroes; and finally, that segment of Northerners who did care, who could be depended upon to help distressed slaves.

Father's face, so animated from the telling of affairs in Boston, grew grave. "I don't know, Charlotte. It's impossible to tell. Some say Burns will be returned to placate the South for our opposition to the Nebraska Bill. It's so bound up in the political situation, but in the end I suppose, comes down to a contest between two men. If Richard Dana can convince Commissioner Loring that under existing law Anthony Burns is entitled to his freedom, and if Loring can be sure that in exercising to the fullest his duty as a United States commissioner—representing both North and South, you understand—there are no grounds for rendering Burns to his master, then he will go free. I quite honestly feel that despite popular sentiment in Boston, Burns doesn't stand much chance."

Glumly we climbed into the carriage. The horse turned up Washington Street.

"Dana, by the way, was quite upset by the rush on the Court House," said Father. "He doesn't condone physical violence as a way of accomplishing things, and he was pretty scornful of that Worcester minister for his part in organizing a mob action."

"Higginson?" mused Mr. Remond. "It doesn't seem to be Higginson's nature to sit on his hands. When he supports something, he does it wholeheartedly. That's how he preached himself out of a pulpit down in Newburyport, speaking his mind about abolition and social reform and a lot of other radical causes until he'd outdistanced the opinions of his congregation. Garrison will employ any method short of physical violence, but Higginson will take the final step as well."

Resistance, nonresistance, higher law, federal law— my head was swimming with theories and opinions I had heard attributed to this faction or that, to one antislavery leader or another, in the past few days. There had even been talk of severing the Union. In my confusion I didn't know any longer what I myself believed. I could admire William Lloyd Garrison, whom my father and grandfather loved so well, and at the same time I could fervently support the half-cocked actions of the Vigilance Committee. I could see the logic of working within the legal structure for the freedom of my race, but the process was endlessly slow, and the road often doubled back upon itself. My heart leapt to the call of allegiance to an overgoverning moral righteousness, but might not this, when carried to extremes or misapplied, lead to national chaos?

It is one thing to know you are right, as I knew to my depths that in this beautiful world no man should be in chains. It is another to act. I was frustrated by wanting to contribute such poor talents as I possessed to the antislavery cause but not knowing what I thought or how I should proceed. One thing was certain. Everything depended upon emancipation of the slave. Once the cursed system was abolished, colored people would know an end to oppression—or so I thought then.

On Tuesday morning Sarah Remond and I took the cars to Boston to attend the second day's antislavery meetings. We found the city outwardly much quieter than we expected, though indignation and excitement were evident. We walked past the Court House, lawlessly converted into a prison and filled with soldiers who looked from the doors and windows with an authoritative insolence that made my blood boil. I felt the strongest contempt for their cowardice and servility, those minions of the South.

It was no secret that the marshal had enlisted as special deputies more than 150 men with the lowest, most despicable reputations in the city. Dana's remark during the trial that Boston crimes had dwindled these past few days because most of its perpetrators were pressed into service at the Court House brought him

roars of laughter. It also brought him soon after a terrible nighttime beating from a ruffian who attacked
him in the dark streets in retaliation for the well-deserved insult.

At Melodeon Hall, where the slavery meetings were
going on, we found the best speakers absent, engaged
in arduous and untiring efforts in behalf of poor
Burns. The hall was well filled, however, with both
colored and white persons, and Sarah pointed out to
me many men and women of whose service to abolition I had heard or read. While we missed the glowing
eloquence of Phillips, Garrison, and Parker, still there
were excellent speeches made, and our hearts responded to the exalted sentiments of truth and liberty
that were uttered. Exciting intelligence occasionally
came from the trial, and this added fresh zeal to the
speakers, of whom the principal were the odd-looking,
vibrant-voiced Stephen S. Foster and his wife, Abigail.
The latter addressed in most eloquent language the
women present, entreating them to urge their husbands and brothers to action, and also to give their aid
on all occasions in our just and holy cause. I did not
see Father the whole day and guessed that he was at
the trial.

We dined that day by invitation, Sarah and I, at the
home of William Lloyd Garrison, and though I could
not say what food lay on my plate or what part of it
found its way into my mouth, I could paint for you the
expression on Mr. Garrison's noble face as we talked of
Burns and of our hopes.

Two men at the table had been in the courtroom all

morning. They informed us that Mr. Dana was building his defense of the fugitive upon two weak spots in the prosecution. In one instance, Colonel Suttle had many months before leased Burns to a neighbor, and it was while in the employ of that neighbor that Burns had escaped. Dana claimed that the neighbor, not Suttle, must therefore be the one to bring suit against the slave. In addition, one of Suttle's witnesses had testified falsely to seeing Burns in Virginia in late March. Dana provided numerous local witnesses to attest to the fact that Burns had been in Boston at that date, and argued that the Southerners did not possess positive identification of their fugitive. It was hoped that these inconsistencies together might be enough for Commissioner Loring to throw the case out of court.

"Do you believe that will happen?" Sarah Remond asked the gentleman who had spoken last.

"Impossible to say," he replied. "Loring is anxious to keep his commission and might therefore overlook Dana's arguments. He's also pretty angry about the death of his deputy during Friday night's fracas. On the other hand, he'll have to withstand a lot of abuse here in the North if he hands over Burns to the South."

"And what of Mr. Burns?" I ventured shyly. "How does he seem to be taking the whole affair?"

"He's frightened, poor devil. Sits as tense and quiet as a frozen rabbit, and doesn't move his head from side to side, but just his eyes."

"The courtroom is full of villains, you've probably heard," added the other man. "Each one has his pockets so bulging and bristling with weapons you'd think you were at the arsenal. There's scarcely room for Burns's supporters at all. Mr. Greenley and I were most fortunate to get in this morning, and as it was, we were questioned and searched for weapons first."

"I suppose," remarked Mrs. Garrison, a saintly-looking woman, "that's because of Friday's attempt at rescuing the prisoner." She sighed. "It does seem to me that it was a mistake."

"You're right, my dear. It has only made matters worse. More militia were brought into the city, a double guard around the Court House. Yes, I quite agree, Mr. Dana's method is the only way. The laws are wrong and shouldn't be obeyed. Yet, neither should we resort to violence." As he spoke, William Garrison looked out over the top of rimless spectacles with the serenity of a professor supporting a classroom theory. There was little in his face or manner to suggest that this man had by his pen and voice done more than any other in America to inflame passions in North and South for or against abolition.

Who could guess to see him that William Garrison had been mobbed and jeered many, many times since he first espoused the cause of antislavery? I am still moved today by the challenge he hurled out in the opening issue of the *Liberator,* the newspaper he founded in 1831 to give voice to his vehement feelings:

Let Southern oppressors tremble—let their secret abettors tremble—let their Northern apologists tremble—let all the enemies of the persecuted blacks tremble. . . . : I *will be* as harsh as truth, and as uncompromising as justice. On this subject I do not wish to think, or speak, or write, with moderation. . . . I am in earnest.—I will not equivocate—I will not excuse—I will not retreat a single inch—AND I WILL BE HEARD.

That was but the first unleashing of Garrison's righteous fury. My grandfather James Forten was among his earliest friends and one of the first subscribers to the *Liberator*. In fact, by rounding up other subscribers in Philadelphia Grandfather helped keep the paper from foundering after its first few issues.

Mr. Garrison's fanatical views on the evil of slavery stemmed from deep religious convictions. His Christian spirit burned bright within him as he addressed all of us gathered that June midday in his dining room. Suddenly, as I listened in near reverence to him speak in support of the nonresistant principles to which he kept firm, I knew that greatly as I admired him I could never agree with him about nonresistance. Unchristian though it might seem, I would stop at nothing to secure a man or woman freedom.

To spin this story longer becomes agony to me. On Friday our worst fears were realized; the decision was against poor Burns, and he was sent back to bondage. Father witnessed the shame of Massachusetts. He stood among fifty thousand angry spectators that infamous afternoon, burning like most of them with helpless wrath and indignation. Buildings near the Court House were draped in mourning. A black coffin

swung from a window across the street. On Boston
Common stood a loaded cannon, while two thousand
soldiers formed an armored corridor lining the streets
from the Court House to Long Wharf, where the dirty
harbor waters slapped the hull of a waiting Virginia-
bound vessel.

In the middle of a moving column of soldiers
walked Anthony Burns incongruously dressed in the
first suit of clothes he had ever owned, bought for him
for his trial. It is said that he looked out over the fixed
rifles of his escort, past cavalry with drawn swords, to
the sea of stricken faces beyond, and commented,
"There sure is a lot of folks to see a colored man walk
through the streets."

The depression that settled upon my spirits that day
and for many days thereafter is still memorable to me.
It seemed but an extension of the cloud hanging over
all our persecuted race. Though the Salem June remained as lovely as before, its charms could
not reach me now. My heart was with Theodore Parker
the following Sunday when he thundered wrath-
fully from his pulpit of the crime committed by Commissioner Loring against the people of Massachusetts. It was at the meeting in Framingham on Independence Day when William Lloyd Garrison burned
first a copy of the Fugitive Slave Law, and then a copy
of Commissioner Loring's decision, and then a copy of
the Grand Jury charge against the Court House assault
leaders, and finally, amid loud shouts of "Amen," a
copy of the Constitution of the United States. That
was July 4, 1854, and on the same occasion a peculiar

friend of Ralph Waldo Emerson's from Concord, a man named Henry David Thoreau, spoke from the platform also, saying, "I feel that my investment in life here is worth many per cent less since Massachusetts last deliberately sent back an innocent man, Anthony Burns, to slavery."

In another, more personal way my dreams were shattered by the Burns affair. Father wrote to me from Philadelphia the following week to say he had decided against moving to Massachusetts. Prejudiced by the outcome of the trial, he said he could not see that New England offered him greater personal liberty than Philadelphia did. Thus ended a plan dear to me.

If any good at all came from the whole event, it was in the legislature's strengthening, a year later, of the Massachusetts personal liberty law. Thereafter application of the Fugitive Slave Law became impossible in the state.

When I was much younger than I am now, I kept a journal for several years, beginning the day of my arrival in Salem. It is to it that I refer these many years later when I feel compelled to draw together my experiences. You may well ask why, for I am not really sure of my purpose in reexamining the pages written so long ago. My life has been full and interesting and in many ways unique, but that is not enough. Perhaps it is because I have always carried pent within me the voice of rebellion against cruelty and injustice to my race, and now at last, like Mr. Garrison, *I will be heard.*

Chapter 2

My grandfather James Forten was born in Philadelphia in poverty in 1766. When he died seventy-six
years later, he was among the wealthiest, most highly
respected citizens in the city.

He was sketchily educated in his youth, for a while
attending the school of the Quaker philanthropist Anthony Benezet. But Grandfather's father died when he
was nine years old, and he had to leave school and find
work to help support his mother and sister. The first
guns of the American Revolution began firing soon
after, and by the time he was fourteen, Grandfather
was begging his mother to let him go to war. When
eventually she relented, he found a place as powder
boy aboard the privateer the *Royal Louis.*

Stephen Decatur, father of the famous naval hero of

the same name, was captain of the *Royal Louis,* and nineteen others of the two hundred men aboard were Negroes. It was an exciting experience for a boy. Sailing from Philadelphia in July 1781, the *Royal Louis* met a British brig-o-war. After a great battle, with blood shed on both sides, the *Royal Louis* captured the enemy vessel and brought it into port. There was great cheering and excitement in the harbor, and years afterward, Grandfather said he still remembered how it felt to be a hero.

The second cruise of the *Royal Louis* was ill fated, however. The American privateer met up with three English warships, was captured, and all aboard the *Royal Louis* were made prisoners of war. Being captured was what my grandfather and his family had dreaded most, for those were still the days of the international slave trade and Negro prisoners were usually sent to the British West Indies and sold into slavery. Grandfather fully expected never to see his home or know freedom again. But by the greatest good fortune the captain of the ship on which Grandfather was held, an Englishman named Sir John Beasley, chose James Forten to be companion to his young son, who was also on board. The two boys were close in age and became friends. Grandfather always claimed he owed his liberty to a game of marbles, for his superiority over young Beasley at that game inspired admiration in the English boy who communicated it to his father. The captain, in turn, decided to prevent such an intelligent, likable Negro from becoming a slave. At first he resolved to take Grandfather to England, where slavery had recently been outlawed and where there was strong agitation to abolish the colonial slave trade entirely. Beasley even offered to pay for James Forten's education, but Grandfather patriotically refused to desert the land of his birth, and Captain Beasley had to follow the only other possible course of action. He put James Forten aboard a prison ship, the *Old Jersey*, with a letter signed by himself requesting that James Forten be exchanged for a British prisoner as soon as possible.

The experience aboard the *Old Jersey* was a ghastly one. My grandfather spent seven months crammed with thousands of other prisoners in the hold of the ship, given rotten food to eat and foul water to drink. Disease ran rampant, with nothing to hinder its course, and many hundreds of men died all around him. As greatly as he suffered, however, Grandfather knew that his experience was still not as terrible as the dreadful "middle passage," the sea voyage endured by captured Africans being taken to the Americas as slaves. At last Grandfather was exchanged and made his way home to his mother, who had thought him dead.

There was one thing Grandfather had had plenty of time to do on the prison ship, and that was to think. He thought about what Captain Beasley had told him of the better life free Negroes might lead in England. He thought about what Philadelphia would be like after the war. Pennsylvania was probably the most enlightened state in America for Negroes. The Quakers had long opposed slavery and had worked for a full century to end slavery within their own sect and within the state. The earliest abolition society had been formed in Pennsylvania. Together Quakers and abolitionists had just brought about a new law guaranteeing more rights to free Negroes. Now Grandfather could be tried in the same courts as a white man, under the same laws, and be given a trial by jury. No other state had such laws. There were new protections, too, for free men of color against being kidnapped across the border into slavery in Virginia or Maryland. But Negroes could not vote, nor was there opportunity for a good education, and until a man can vote and learn, he has no real way of bettering his life. He and his family will always be second-class citizens. The question in Grandfather's mind was, Might things really be different in England? Grandfather decided he would go there to find out.

Shortly after the Revolution ended, therefore, James Forten and his brother-in-law signed onto the crew of a merchant ship headed for Liverpool. For a year they worked on the waterfront, first in Liverpool, then in London, and drank in the scenes and atmosphere of England following the Revolution. James Forten found that in England as in America, it was the Quakers who were pushing for reforms for Negroes, and the Quakers had been inspired by the writings of his old teacher, Anthony Benezet. Grandfather was not yet twenty years old, and what he saw and heard of zealous English reformers such as Granville Sharp, who vigorously opposed slavery and the slave trade, made a great impression on him. He listened to Sharp's plans for establishing a colony for newly freed Negroes on the coast of Africa, and he marveled at the growing concern among Englishmen for the plight of the enslaved African. He admired, too, the established political institutions and legal traditions through which Britishers could work to see slavery abolished. In contrast, America had just been through a violent upheaval. It had no federal political institutions, though a convention was just then taking place in Philadelphia to set up a united government and draft a constitution.

Despite the attractions of England, Grandfather could not turn his back on the hope and promise of his own country. Strong sentiments concerning the rights of men were in the air there, and James Forten had hope that the guarantees to life and liberty might include Negroes and might sound the death knell for slavery. He must have been encouraged when a short time later tax-paying Negroes in Pennsylvania were given the right to vote. But the Constitutional Convention, which finished its incredible historic labor at the end of the long, hot summer of 1787, wrote into the United States Constitution a compromise phrase that was to cause trouble for almost a century. The presence of slaves was tacitly acknowledged by a reference to "all other persons," but no rights were guaranteed them. Eventually there would be people who would disown the Constitution and cry for disunion because of that simple phrase.

Strong patriotism led James Forten back to the United States afire with desire and determination to work for the freedom of his own people. In Philadelphia he became apprenticed to a sailmaker named Robert Bridges, whose loft edged the bustling city docks along the Delaware River. He was so industrious and capable that he soon was made foreman of the loft, and twelve years later when Mr. Bridges retired, Grandfather became the owner. By that time Grandfather had developed a device for more efficiently handling the huge, heavy, unwieldy canvas sails, a worthy invention which he patented and which eventually brought him wealth. Meanwhile, he married my grandmother and sired eight children. The second was my father, Robert Bridges Forten.

What a busy, exciting place the Forten sail loft was! My father, who operated the business for several years after Grandfather's death, often took me along with him on Saturday mornings when I was a little girl. I would sit atop a high stool at the clerk's desk and add rows of figures, or copy neat, careful entries into the ledger for Father, feeling enormously important and helpful. The ground floor was quite dark, for the building was hemmed in by neighboring warehouses, but a glowing wood stove made cheery warmth, and the pungent odor of wood tar, emanating from supplies stored in the rear, created a special and unforgettably pleasant atmosphere. Customers who came to order sails or buy canvas, cordage, hardware, fittings, and other marine materials would compliment Father on his attractive helper, and Father would say yes, women were certainly making their way in the world these days, and the customers would laugh, or if they could catch my eye, they'd wink.

The real work of the loft went on in the huge open room upstairs where giant sheets of cotton canvas were unrolled across the floor, then cut to match a pattern that had been outlined on the floor with strips of tin. Every sail was different. In fact the trickiest part of sailmaking came at the very beginning when two men skilled at measuring had to board the ship requiring new sails, climb the rigging, and measure the masts and yards to determine what size was needed. Father always said that moving around the shrouds and rat-lines high off the deck of a vessel took special sea legs, and whenever he did it himself, he was always glad the ship was anchored in the river and not tossing about at sea.

Once the measurements were known and the sail sketched in small scale on paper, tin strips would be nailed to the floor to outline the precise dimensions. The man who did the cutting could feel the tin through the dense canvas sheet and cut to the proper size. The enormous sail occupied most of the floor, so that the wood stove had to be hung from the ceiling. Someone mounted a ladder from time to time to keep it fed.

There was one matter on which Grandfather was very particular. He refused to use American canvas, the cotton for which had been grown in the South by slaves. He bought instead Egyptian cotton, brought in by trade ship, and stored it in enormous heavy bolts on the first floor of the loft. After it had been unrolled and cut, the sails had to be hemmed and fitted with grommets. Bolt rope was stitched along the edges of the sail for added strength, and more fittings fixed to that. For sewing the men used awls to punch the holes, and big three-sided needles and leather palms that provided a hard surface against which to push the needle through the stiff canvas. What huge hands and arm muscles those sailmakers had from wrestling with the coarse, heavy fabric! Grandfather employed about forty men, both Negro and white, and it was always interesting to me to watch them work. Under their powerful fingers the splicing of rope, the stitching of sail, seemed a delightfully gross exaggeration of the sewing circles that I was more familiar with.

Life along the wharves was never dull. Boats of every size and description moved up and down the river. Workers loaded and unloaded them, hauled and fetched, lifted and piled. The decks swarmed with motion, as did the humming shipyards. Men of business bustled here and there—in at the Custom House, out at the shipbuilder's, in at the fish market, out at the cooper's. Commerce was in the air, the jingle and hum of buying and selling and transactions being made, and a sense of urgency pervaded the area. People arrived and departed Philadelphia by boat. With them came and went the latest news. Imports, exports, raw materials, manufactured goods, seafood, and farm produce were all transported by water route. Everywhere activity met the eye, cacophony the ear, and pervasive odors of fish and salt water filled the nostrils. Above the whole scene wheeled hundreds of seagulls, diving and squawking, seeming to personify the motion and excitement of the waterfront.

Grandfather was something of a local hero along the docks. On several occasions, all during the winter months, he jumped into the river fully clothed to rescue men from drowning. He never could understand why sailors and dockhands undertook their vocation without first learning how to swim. The Philadelphia Humane Society eventually awarded James Forten a plaque that hung for many years in our Lombard Street parlor, "testimony of its approbation of his meritorious conduct and successful exertions in rescuing, at the imminent hazard of his life, four persons from drowning in the River Delaware." He later rescued three others.

Grandfather also played a heroic part in organizing two thousand Negro citizens to build redoubts at the mouth of the Schuylkill River, south of Philadelphia, in 1812 when British gunboats were attacking along the eastern seacoast. Fortunately the defenses were never needed, but Philadelphians were grateful for the patriotic efforts of their colored citizens.

The number of free Negroes in the North was steadily growing. There were several reasons why. One by one, the Northern states abolished slavery within their borders, and these free Negroes increased by the natural process of having children who had more children. Negroes were occasionally freed in the South, too, but were not wanted there, some states forbidding them by law to remain after they were freed. They made their way to Northern cities. Runaway slaves also steadily added to the increase.

Pennsylvania was especially hospitable to fugitives,

for its Quakers and abolitionists worked tirelessly to aid the black man. By passing laws, writing petitions and pamphlets, forming vigilance committees to aid escaped slaves and to track kidnapped free Negroes, they encouraged freedmen and slaves to seek refuge in Pennsylvania. But at the same time that there was active Northern sympathy for slaves, a strange inversion occurred, perhaps more clearly evident in Pennsylvania than elsewhere. While white men might generally abhor slavery and be sympathetic toward its victims, white men also possessed little love for the free Negro because of the problems he created. Southern freedmen and fugitives, usually ignorant and destitute, immigrated in increasing numbers into Northern cities, swelling the slum areas. Unable to procure adequate shelter, food, and clothing, they lived in wretched circumstances. Accustomed to menial jobs, of which there were not enough to go around, many Negroes could not find employment, and this made them appear shiftless and unself-sufficient in the eyes of many white citizens. The jobless, desperate Negroes all too often turned to lawlessness. As crime rates increased in the cities, so did white prejudice against free Negroes. They were a nuisance, an undesirable social burden, and something had to be done about them.

In 1813 a bill was introduced in the Pennsylvania legislature to keep free Negroes from entering the state. Since the bill challenged the rights of the free Negroes already living in Pennsylvania, it stirred my grandfather to action.

James Forten had grown prominent among the Negroes of Philadelphia as a man respected for his intelligence, kindliness, generosity, and talent for natural leadership. He was an ardent abolitionist and a founding member of the first Negro church in the city, which served as the earliest rallying point for the colored people. He had dared to raise his voice on behalf of black men on the second day of the new century— in January 1800—by signing a petition to Congress urging changes in the Fugitive Slave Act of 1793. His petition created quite a stir in the House of Representatives but eventually died in committee.

Now, in 1813, James Forten was determined to do more than endorse an ill-fated petition. On behalf of the Negro citizens of Pennsylvania, he wrote and published *A Series of Letters by a Man of Color*. Few Negroes before him had dared publish their views, especially such advanced views as Grandfather held, for he believed firmly that there was no biological difference between the black and white races. His was one of the earliest Negro voices crying in the wilderness.

"Has the God who made the white man and the black left any record declaring us a different species?" he wrote. "Are we not sustained by the same power, supported by the same food, hurt by the same wounds, wounded by the same wrongs, pleased with the same delights, and propagated by the same means? And should we not then enjoy the same liberty, and be protected by the same laws? . . ."

His voice was lifted against the commonly held theory behind which Americans hid their shame of slavery and their hatred of free black men, the theory that the Negro was naturally inferior—physically and intellectually inferior. But the Declaration of Independence declared that all men are created equal. Why, then, argued James Forten, should free Negroes, some of whom had roots in America that extended as far back as any white man's, some of whom had served in the Revolutionary War and the War of 1812, why should they be excluded from the benefits accorded all Americans, why should they not have liberty to live where they wanted and to work toward solving their problems?

The bill before the Pennsylvania legislature was eventually defeated, perhaps in part because of James Forten's appeal, perhaps because a new solution to the free Negro problem was gaining popularity. Colonization, the idea of founding a special colony where Negroes might go to live by themselves and establish their own government and way of life, was not a new idea. English abolitionists had advocated it decades earlier. But now it was greeted with fresh enthusiasm by many Northerners and Southerners as the way to be rid of this increasing, unwanted segment of the population, the Negro nonslaves, who seemingly had no chance for racial development in this country.

In order to make colonization appealing to Negroes, the idea had to be clothed in persuasive argument. Colonization was to provide the opportunity for the Negro to establish a successful life for himself. Many well-intentioned abolitionists sincerely believed in this positive aspect of colonization and gave support to it. The American Colonization Society, organized late in

1816, was given money by the federal government with which it bought land on the west coast of Africa and founded Liberia. The first shipload of American Negroes landed there in 1820. Free Negroes throughout the North were encouraged to follow, and many did. Negroes in the South were manumitted, or freed, by sympathetic masters on condition that they would go to Liberia to live. Altogether, by mid-century, nearly eight thousand American Negroes were relocated in Liberia.

But the vast majority of black people in this country had no interest in leaving the United States, so that the colonizationists encountered strong resistance among the very people they proposed to help. Father told me how Grandfather Forten was approached by founders of the society and offered a responsible position in the Liberian government if he would go. He adamantly refused and instead, early in 1817, helped convene a meeting of Philadelphia Negroes to pass resolutions against the plan "to exile us from the land of our nativity."

A few days later he headed another convention at which three thousand Negroes endorsed an "Address to the Humane and Benevolent Inhabitants of the City and County of Philadelphia." The address insisted that peopling Liberia with ex-slaves and the least desirable free Negroes—those who were uneducated, untrained, and devoid of religious instruction—would blight the new colony in Africa and at the same time would encourage the kidnapping and deporting of free Negroes in this country and it would force the price of slaves higher. Despite such vociferous objections, a branch of the American Colonization Society took root in the city of Philadelphia, and the whole movement found firm support throughout the North.

I need not recount all the words and deeds that filled the life of this beloved, humane gentleman, my grandfather, to convince you that he devoted himself to his family and his fellow men. The middle years of his life were active, earnestly directed, and rewarding. He raised and educated eight children—four sons and four daughters—in itself no small feat. The hospitality of his home was extended to numerous relatives and near relatives, so that there were periods when as many as twenty persons gathered regularly for family meals. Visiting abolitionists were frequent guests at table, and family conversation turned on the endlessly fascinating subject of antislavery.

To remember how my father talked of home during his boyhood causes me to marvel at my grandmother, who kept such a large household running, with every meal looming large as a Christmas banquet, and the thought of the sewing and darning and washing and ironing and canning and pickling and dusting and sweeping is absolutely staggering to the imagination. Of course, with four daughters and numerous female relatives the duties were not hers alone. Yet she must plan and manage and keep all household affairs moving smoothly, and I think her performance must easily have rivaled my grandfather's command of his forty sailmakers.

The concerns of the growing Negro community

were my grandfather's also, and together with Reverend Absalom Jones, Robert Douglas, Francis Perkins, Reverend Richard Allen, and other Negro leaders in Philadelphia, he worked to establish Negro churches, Negro schools, Negro libraries, debating societies, newspapers, benevolent societies, and charities in the city. Gradually through institutions such as these, the free Negroes began to acquire a sense of identity and of status in Philadelphia and started to cope with their own problems.

Education, of course, was the key. How thoroughly James Forten must have agreed with his fellow free Negro David Walker who, in a famous and vociferous *Appeal to the Colored Citizens of the World,* cried in 1829, "I would crawl on my hands and knees through mud and mire to the feet of a learned man, where I would sit and humbly supplicate him to instil into me that which neither devils nor tyrants could remove, only with my life—for colored people to acquire learning in this country makes tyrants quake and tremble on their sandy foundation."

Education was the bootstrap by which the poor, ignorant Negro could pull himself up in the world, could leave bondage and the slums. Yet how heartbreaking a task it was, for the slave states forbade by law the teaching of an A, B, or C to a slave, and even the free states closed to colored people the public schools available to white children. Any opportunity for Negroes to associate with learned men came only through the printed page. Well, no matter, a free colored man must start his own schools, must secure his own tutors for his children, and find books for them, too, all of which James Forten was fortunate enough to be able to do. But he could not so easily conquer the next step, for when his sons were of an age to learn a trade, there was no one in the city of Philadelphia or round about willing to apprentice them. James, Jr., and Robert, who leaned toward mathematics, were taken into the sail loft and learned that business from bottom to top. The next two sons at first followed suit, but later drifted to other occupations in other parts of the country, and I never knew them. My aunts, at least the three who remained in Philadelphia, were remarkable women. Aunt Margaretta founded her own school for Negro children and ran it for many years with great success. Aunt Harriet married Robert Purvis—a wonderful man of whom I will tell more shortly—and raised a large family. Aunt Sarah remained at home and took charge of the household in which I grew up. All three were active and forceful in the effort to end slavery.

James Forten's interests extended beyond the family and the civic scene, however. Temperance, women's rights, universal peace—there was no end of ways in which the condition of men and women might be perfected. And that theme, the perfectibility of man, his infinite capacity for improving his lot and freeing himself from insidious shackles of every variety, was the message of the age, the message that informed the Constitution of the United States and the Bill of Rights. How far short of the ideal men fell in actuality! Well, James Forten would do his part to rectify the world by founding the American Moral Reform Society, a Negro organization dedicated to every right and good cause that needed support. The rightest and goodest and most demanding cause of all, however, escaped the confines of the Moral Reform Society and demanded an organization and effort all its own. That was anti-slavery.

The efforts of the Pennsylvania Abolition Society had never ceased, and Grandfather and many of his friends had, over the years, concerned themselves with petitions and protest meetings and resolutions directed against colonization and toward gradual emancipation of the slaves. But about the year 1830, at a time when James Forten had entered his sixties and had amassed a fortune of over a hundred thousand dollars, a new energy seized the abolition movement. That energy was invested in the person of a single man who was determined that slavery in the United States should end immediately. Not eventually, not gradually, but at once and for all.

Perhaps every cause if it is to succeed needs one fanatic, one person so inspired by the rightness of what he believes that he will go through fire for his ideals. For abolitionists, that man was William Lloyd Garrison, whose uncompromising belief in the wrongness of slavery and uncompromising efforts to end it were a chief reason the slaves were eventually freed. Garrison devoted his life to bringing about emancipation by writing, by publishing, by speaking, by organizing, antislavery societies. He hurled out invective and thrived on the unpopularity it earned him. He pointed an accusing finger at some of the most sacred institutions in America—at the clergy, at political parties, at the Constitution, and at honored men. He could suffer no views but his own and managed to make enemies even among the supporters of his cause, but there is no doubt in the end of his effectiveness. Through it all, he called himself a pacifist, a nonresistant, who believed in the moral argument rather than the fist.

I had learned from Father of Garrison's early life. Born in poverty in Newburyport, Massachusetts, abandoned by his father at an early age and separated from his mother not much later, William Lloyd Garrison struggled through childhood, and during adolescence learned the printer's trade. By the time he was twenty-four years old, he had briefly been editor of no fewer than four newspapers—in Newburyport, Boston, Bennington, Vermont, and Baltimore. Garrison possessed a natural passion for reform, for correcting the evils of the world, and in his editorials he attacked the drinking of liquor, gambling, prostitution, and breaking the Sabbath, and he championed abolition and women's rights. His partner in the Baltimore enterprise was a dedicated abolitionist named Benjamin Lundy. Together they published the *Genius of Universal Emancipation,* whose message you may guess. Garrison's opinions soon outstripped Lundy's, however. Garrison did not think freeing the slaves should be a gradual process, allowing time for education and adjustment to the white man's ways. Delay would simply prolong slavery indefinitely. The slaves should be freed immediately, and all at once. The great shock of adjustment for both black and white was but the price to be paid for becoming involved in the nefarious system in the first place. Furthermore, Garrison thought, colonization was only a temporary expedient, not a solution to the slavery problem at all. Before long, Garrison found himself jailed in Baltimore for libel, having pointed his finger in print at a Newburyport merchant whom he accused of trafficking in slaves.

After his short prison term ended, Garrison parted with Benjamin Lundy and made his way to Boston. There in 1830 he launched the *Liberator,* the newspaper through which his vociferous clamor for emancipation never ceased until the Civil War ended thirty-five years later. During the next few years Garrison also published an influential attack on colonization and founded the New England Anti-Slavery Society, an organization that claimed immediate emancipation as one of its goals, thus distinguishing itself from the slower, more gradual efforts of prior abolition societies. In a very short time Garrison's name was known in the North and reviled in the South, and his newspaper and pamphlets were banned in many Southern states.

It was always surprising to people that a man who was so belligerent and uncompromising and even offensive in print and on the lecture platform was, in personal meeting, the mildest and most pleasant of acquaintances. Small and neat in appearance, with head bald and eyes twinkling behind narrow spectacles, Lloyd Garrison was a kindly person whom it was difficult not to like. Certainly my grandfather felt the warmest affection and admiration for him. He was a guest many times in our home in Philadelphia.

Without doubt Forten and Garrison influenced one another. My grandfather's firm conviction that no biological inferiority separated the black and white races, and his scorn for the colonization scheme confirmed Garrison's thinking on these subjects. In turn Garrison's belief that the way to bring about abolition of slavery and to end oppression of free Negroes was through peaceful nonresistance and moral suasion strengthened James Forten's own faith in the basic goodness of man and the eventual triumph of righteousness.

Grandfather's desire that his fellow free Negroes elevate themselves and show white men through precept and example that given an opportunity, Negroes would prove themselves as intelligent, as moral, and as useful to society as any white citizen speaks plainly through his writings. I still have his pamphlets and petitions and protests and proposals, as well as those appeals to the free colored inhabitants of the country issued through the annual national Negro conventions of the 1830's in which he played a leading role. His rhetoric is anguished, forceful, and clear. It flowed again in 1832, as it had in 1813, when the Pennsylvania legislature once more tried to keep free Negroes and fugitives out of Pennsylvania, and when it denied free Negroes accused of being runaways the right to trial by jury. By 1832 Grandfather and his fellow petitioners were able to point with pride to the many educational, religious, and charitable improvements the

Philadelphia Negroes had made in their community, the vast strides that had been made against all odds. He had such conviction that the eyes of white men would one day be opened to the error of their prejudice and false judgment against the blacks that often he must have been cruelly disappointed that the Negro continued to be spat upon, legislated against, and occasionally mobbed. All too often it seemed that the harder blacks worked to improve, the more limited were their opportunities outside the Negro community.

Garrison's belief in the powers of moral exhortation went far beyond Grandfather's. Garrison's rhetoric exceeded the bounds of polished restraint. His credo of nonresistance eventually went as far as a refusal to support political parties because they all compromised to some degree on the subject of abolition.

It extended to refusing to vote and then to refusing to support the Constitution and urging others to do likewise. Spurring nonresistance to its limit, Garrison called the Constitution of the United States "a covenant with death and an agreement with hell." No UNION WITH SLAVEHOLDERS became his battle cry.

One of the greatest blows against the free Negroes in Pennsylvania happened in 1837, just a few years before Grandfather's death. The State Constitutional Convention took from Negroes the right to vote, a privilege enjoyed in Pennsylvania since 1790. James Forten helped call together a great meeting to endorse an appeal to the state's white population from its forty thousand Negroes. Seven men had prepared the appeal.

One was James Forten's son Robert; another was his son-in-law Robert Purvis. Like James Forten, their faith in the power of words, logic, and eloquent sarcasm to persuade their oppressors resulted in sinewy, moving rhetoric that could, alas, make no headway against a force unspoken and illogical, the force of ignorant, fearful prejudice.

When you have taken from an individual his right to vote, you have made the government, in regard to him, a mere despotism; and you have taken a step toward making it a despotism to all. . . . Fellow citizens, if there is one of us who has abused the right of suffrage, let him be tried and punished according to law. But in the name of humanity, in the name of justice, in the name of the God you profess to worship, who has no respect of persons, do not turn into gall and wormwood the friendship we bear to yourselves by ratifying a Constitution which tears from us a privilege dearly earned and inestimably prized.

The words were penned in vain by my uncle Robert Purvis, chairman of the appeal committee, and a man who was as deeply involved in abolitionist activities as my grandfather, and who, like him, was a respected gentleman and admired leader of the Negro community. James Forten loved Robert Purvis as a son, and had earnestly blessed his marriage to his daughter Harriet.

Uncle Robert was strikingly handsome. He was tall

and of so fair a complexion he might easily have passed for white. "A voluntary Negro," I've heard him called. Yet he chose to acknowledge his Negro blood and to fight the black man's fight. Actually his mother was a freeborn woman of Moorish-Jewish extraction, and his father a wealthy English merchant who settled in Charleston, South Carolina, and at his death left Uncle Robert a large inheritance. Uncle Robert settled on a farm at a place named Byberry, a few miles west of Philadelphia. There he and Aunt Harriet lived with their five children, and there Uncle Robert raised some very fine cattle that were forever taking prizes at state and local agricultural shows.

Byberry was my second home throughout my childhood. When the Lombard Street house seemed too big and empty for me to bear, I could step aboard a boat at the foot of Chestnut Street and within an hour and a half be met by Uncle Robert's carriage at the wharf at Andalusia. Once at Byberry, my cousins Hattie and Robert would make life so gay with their chatter and laughter and goings-on that I would altogether forget I was a motherless only child who sometimes talked to herself for company.

Robert, Jr., was my favorite cousin. He resembled his father in light coloring and good looks, but was very boyish and lighthearted, always joking and teasing and fooling. Yet he had a sober side. He read a great deal and could quote Dickens or Shakespeare or the Book of Revelation as occasion demanded, which made him a delightful companion. Like his father, young Robert was an excellent public speaker and early had occasion to orate before antislavery audiences. The only cloud that hung on the bright horizon of his future was a fear of consumption. Of the thin frame and nervous temperament that courts lung disease, he admitted to a dread that fate was directing him toward an early grave. But high spirits generally outlawed morbidity in his lively personality, and nothing delighted me more than to be decked out in Hattie's riding habit and set upon her horse to accompany Robert over the fields and roads surrounding Byberry.

Byberry was a beautiful estate, with a handsome house, stately trees, and wide lawns. The livestock barns and other outbuildings were neat and well kept, the orchards and fields obviously prosperous, and the rolling countryside and woods pleasurable to see. Uncle Robert was the second largest taxpayer in the township and was a popular and admired man. You might imagine his indignation when it was decided that his children might attend the public school but must sit apart from the white children. The three youngest Purvises—two boys and a girl—were darker than Hattie and Robert, and were made to suffer proportionally more slights and insults. Uncle Robert's reaction to the segregation of his children was to keep them at home, set Hattie to tutoring them in their lessons, and refuse to pay his school taxes. Inside of a year either that action had had a significant enough effect on the local pursestrings or Uncle Robert's powers of persuasion were such that he won the day, for the public schools in the area were formally desegregated.

Robert Purvis' retort to the overtures of the Colonization Society—that other threat to his status as freeman and American—was no less outspoken: "I elect to stay on the soil on which I was born, and on the plot of land which I have fairly bought and honestly paid for. Don't advise me to leave, and don't add insult to injury by telling me it's for my own good; of that I am to be the judge."

Perhaps the reason I most admired Uncle Robert was that he was a man of action. After all, it is one thing to talk, to sway people by eloquence to this cause or that, as any clergyman can demonstrate. It is another to be willing to risk your skin for your principles and for other human beings. Always I have reserved my greatest love for those willing to brave physical danger for their beliefs. There were many such noble men among the abolitionists.

Uncle Robert earned the local title, "President of the Underground Railroad," by his efforts to help runaway slaves. He helped to organize and head the Philadelphia Vigilance Committee, and especially after the passage of the Fugitive Slave Bill of 1850, assisted in literally hundreds of escapes. While I was never party to any of the negotiations, young Robert knew of them and sometimes participated in hiding and speeding frightened fugitives from bondage north to Canada. As far as I know, no fugitive was ever apprehended while in Uncle Robert's custody, though knowledge of his involvement in the underground railroad was not entirely secret.

But I have skipped ahead in recounting my grandfather's history. That eminent gentleman passed from the scene in February 1842, dying in a peaceful and happy state of mind, content that he had done what he could on earth to help his fellow men and that God was about to receive him joyfully into His kingdom.

I was but a child of four at the time, yet memories of his funeral remain among the scraps of my childhood memories. I remember a vast crowd marching in procession behind the seemingly enormous box that held my grandfather, all frigid and hard now to the touch. I later learned that over two thousand colored people and many hundred white persons followed his coffin to the African Episcopal Church of St. Thomas, which James Forten had helped to found. There they joined in public tribute to this patriarch and truly excellent man.

The emotions of childhood are curiously out of joint. I recall feeling sadder about Grandfather than I had when my canary died, yet not so desolate as a time shortly thereafter when Father left on a journey of several months, for at Grandfather's funeral there were scores of friends and relatives dispensing love and solace to all of us in the Lombard Street household. There was, too, a peculiar note of joy, as if the life of this superior man supplied fine reason for rejoicing, whereas when Father went away, I was simply and unutterably alone.

Of all the tributes paid James Forten I like this one, published shortly after his funeral: "Thus died this truly eminent man. Eminent for his industry, eminent for his talents, eminent for his moral sensibilities. . . . Oh that all our young men would imitate his example and endeavor to maintain such an unblemished character as he possessed, even to the day of his death." So read his obituary in Garrison's *Liberator*.

Chapter 3

~·~·~·~·~·~·~·~·~·~·~·~·~·~·~·~·~·~·~·

During my youth, children were quite commonly "brought up on the Bible," nourished from a tender age by the ponderous rhetoric of the Old Testament, inspired by the poetic cadences of the New. I knew the Bible as well as any other child, yet it was not what nourished me.

On the shelves of Grandfather's library were some volumes I found and devoured before I was ten. If the New Testament could instruct "Remember them that are in bonds as bound with them," I found unforgettable the sufferings of American slaves depicted in Grandfather's books. One, called *American Slavery As It Is,* contained accounts of over a thousand incidents involving slaves. In it I read of beatings, squalid living conditions, heart-rending separations of husband from wife and of child from mother, of brutal labor, and the cruel, inhuman treatment that was the lot of the black man in chains. The book's ugly, horrible details surfeited my imagination and overwhelmed my emotions. I felt an anguished numbness at the plight of those hapless souls. There, but for the grace of God, went I.

Burned into my memory was the testimonial of a young Northerner who spent a year as tutor and preacher on a Sea Island plantation in South Carolina. He described a scene at the family breakfast table when a female house slave poured too much molasses on the plate of one of the white children. The child's father, owner and master of the plantation, used this minor accident as pretext for a severe beating. Before the eyes of his family and the Northern tutor, the master pinned the house servant's hands and began to beat her about the head. Then his ire mounted sufficiently that he removed his shoe and went about striking the poor slave with that until she fell sobbing to the floor. Still he beat her until satisfied that he had repaid her for her clumsiness. To the amazement of the horrified Northerner, the servant later returned to the dining room, cut, bruised and swollen, to thank her master for teaching her a lesson.

Later under very different circumstances I visited that plantation on St. Helena Island. Still later and again under very different circumstances I became related by marriage to the author of *American Slavery As It Is,* the Reverend Theodore Dwight Weld.

But Weld's wasn't the only nourishing volume I found on Grandfather's shelves. I found David Walk-

er's *Appeal*, which urged the slaves to rise against their
masters, to win by force and bloodshed what could be
won in no other way. It was a terrifying book, not only
to a little girl reading it in the corner of a dimly lit library, but to slaveholders who had reason to live in
dread of slave uprisings. Father told me that David
Walker's *Appeal* was banned in the South, and that because of it some states had passed harsher laws against
educating slaves and against permitting blacks to
gather together. David Walker died mysteriously a
year after his book was published. Some said he was
murdered.

A different appeal, far more learned, was written by
a white woman named Lydia Maria Child. Mrs. Child
had written several best-selling books about housekeeping, but suddenly she marshaled her talents to
produce *An Appeal in Favor of That Class of Americans Called Africans.* Her book traced the history of
my race and the history of slavery. It described the
horrors of the slave ships and the auction block. It
sought biological and intellectual status for blacks. It
argued against the economics of slavery and urged political abolition of the system. It was a reasoned, reasonable, fervent appeal, and for her trouble Mrs. Child
was reviled in the North and in the South.

You might think these odd volumes for a child to
find interesting, yet they were absorbing to me. The
Negroes in the South were my Israelites in Egypt. I
suffered with their trials and rejoiced in their defend-
ers. The documents, petitions, and slave narratives on
Grandfather's bookshelves made me yearn to help the

slaves. How I longed to write stirring words of prose or verse, words that would strike terror into the hearts of the wicked and inspire the good to espouse the antislavery cause!

My most secret desire was to become a writer, to command with my pen. But when I tried, my little fictions seemed awkward and lifeless. What did I know about screams and lashes? My experience was with slights and insults, with being barred from public conveyances and public places. These were trifles compared to the great public wrongs slaves were obliged to endure, even though they taught a colored child early lessons in distrust and suspicion.

The kind of book I longed to write would paint the whole ugly picture of slavery and prejudice. It would have enough human sympathy to ensnare the most indifferent Northerner and to reform the basest slaveholder. But a far more powerful pen than mine was already at work producing such a book. In 1852 that incendiary masterpiece, _Uncle Tom's Cabin,_ burst like a rocket above the nation, showering sparks into every corner of the land. Humbly I locked my feeble manuscripts away, and like millions in this nation and abroad, paid homage to its author, Harriet Beecher Stowe, the little woman who so wanted everyone to feel "what an accursed thing is slavery."

Mrs. Stowe's tale of the fugitive slave Eliza, fleeing to freedom across the breaking ice of the Ohio River to prevent separation from her small son, of her risky passage northward to Canada with her husband along the underground railroad, of the tragic fate of kind, pious Uncle Tom who journeyed in the other direction, being sold to slaveowners deeper and deeper into the South until he fell into the hands of the cruel overseer Simon Legree and met a pitiful end, stirred the hearts of thousands in the land. The book was printed and reprinted. It was serialized and read in installments before family fires. It was translated into twenty languages and transposed into a popular play. Mrs. Stowe became a celebrity. Everywhere she traveled crowds surrounded her in adulation, to see her, to touch her.

There were many in the South who reviled Mrs. Stowe for exposing the cruelties of the slave system. There were Northerners who felt she had been too kind, had sympathized too much with the tender feelings of slaveowners. Mrs. Stowe claimed to know the people upon whom she based her fictional characters. Such fugitives had passed through Cincinnati, a borderline city, where her house was a stop on the underground railroad. She was acquainted with some kindly, humane slaveowners in Kentucky and had put them in her book. Actually she had created the brightest possible picture of the South's "peculiar institution," but in exploring the dark conflict between slavery and freedom, she had bared many facets of the national conscience and amply illustrated that slavery and freedom could not exist under one flag. Thanks in large part to Mrs. Stowe, slavery became a national issue, rather than a sectional or personal one, after 1852.

Although I had read about fugitive slaves, and while growing up, had heard members of our household talk about desperate escapes, I had never met a fugitive. That opportunity became mine when I had been in Salem with the Remonds just a few months. To their home came a Negro abolitionist named William Wells Brown, a handsome man about my father's age who had just returned from five years' exile in England. He stayed with the Remonds for several weeks, and during his visit he told us his life story, a dark forbidding tale. Because of its incredible hardship and adventure, and because Mr. Brown's experiences illustrate so well the sufferings of the poor slaves, I shall recount here the events of his life just as he told them to us during evenings before the Remond parlor fire.

He had been born a slave, in what year he knew not, but about 1816. His father was a white man, as his light mulatto coloring attested, and his mother a slave. Since by law the child of a slave mother was a slave, no matter who the father might be, William grew up a pale-skinned Negro condemned to be a life-long chattel like many another half-white child on Southern plantations.

William was called just William, for he didn't adopt the name of his father or of his owner as some slaves did. He lived first in the slave cabins of the Lexington, Kentucky, farm where he was born, tumbling, wrestling, and scrambling for bits of food with all the other naked slave urchins, who were watched over by an old woman while the children's mothers worked in the fields. When his master moved to a Missouri farm, William was put to work doing chores under the gaze of a tyrannical, whip-wielding overseer.

About the time William entered his teens and was capable of man's work, his master moved to St. Louis and began a pattern of hiring William out to steamboat captains during the navigation season and putting him to work on farms near the city betweentimes. St. Louis in 1828 was a thriving, rough, frontier river port on the west bank of the Mississippi River. Beyond it stretched the vast Louisiana territory. Great trails leading settlers into the sparsely settled western plains began at St. Louis. Missouri was a slave state, and St. Louis a center for brisk trade up and down the Mississippi, as well as a rounding-up point for slave drivers taking their manacled, chained gangs of Negroes farther south to be sold onto rice, cotton, and sugar plantations.

William's work aboard the riverboats was often back-breaking, his hours long and the cargo heavy, yet he found life on the river exhilarating. Eventually he became a steward, and his duties were lighter, although the treatment he received varied according to the personality of each individual steamboat captain. Between navigation seasons William came under the control of various overseers on the farms where he labored. Once, for a misdemeanor, he was beaten fifty stripes with a cowhide, and his raw body smoked for a while with tobacco leaves in a smokehouse. There was, however, a period of a few months when he was leased to a printer who treated him kindly. The printer was Elijah P. Lovejoy, then editor of the *St. Louis Observer*.

Lovejoy, a young man from Maine, had originally

been an ordained Presbyterian minister. His fierce antislavery sentiments were decidedly out of place in St. Louis, a slave town dominated by Southern businessmen. Lovejoy took an interest in the colored boy, William, who helped keep the premises clean, ran errands, carried type, and did a hundred other chores in the busy printshop. Defying the law that forbade teaching slaves to read and write, Lovejoy found odd hours in which to instruct William. Though the job with Lovejoy lasted only eighteen months, William never forgot the editor's kindness, and he used every small opportunity to practice his reading and writing skills in secret. After leaving Lovejoy's printshop, William never saw the printer again, but he later heard about him, just as everyone in America did, for Elijah P. Lovejoy soon became a martyr to the cause of antislavery.

Lovejoy's career in St. Louis was short-lived. He began to publish a religious journal in which he wrote reckless editorials attacking slavery and urging immediate emancipation. He raised such a storm of wrath against himself that a mob attacked his printshop, destroyed his press, and forced him to flee by night across the Mississippi.

Lovejoy set up new editorial offices in Alton, Illinois, a town ostensibly free but one doing business with slaveholding states and dependent on them for profit. Here Lovejoy's outspoken opinions were no more welcome than they had been in St. Louis. Once, twice, thrice, he was threatened, his family menaced, his offices attacked, and his printing press thrown into the Mississippi. Each time friends and sympathizers helped him reestablish his newspaper and buy new machinery. Lovejoy finally went before a meeting of Alton citizens to plead for his rights and for freedom of the press. Facing a hostile audience he appealed to them, "You come together for the purpose of driving out a confessedly innocent man for no cause but that he dares to think as his conscience and God dictates. . . . If the civil authorities refuse to protect me, I must look to God, and if I die am determined to make my grave in Alton."

Lovejoy's fourth printing press arrived in Alton one middle of the night in early November 1837. Friends helped him move it to a warehouse, where they defended it against his clamorous enemies through that night and the next day. But the second night a mob that was determined to get rid of Lovejoy and his presses once and for all attacked the warehouse, set it afire, and shot at several figures silhouetted inside against the blaze. Elijah Lovejoy fell dead.

It was a shot heard round the world, especially in New England where pulpits rang and editorial pages sizzled with tribute to the martyr who had died for antislavery and freedom of the press. At a great meeting in Faneuil Hall a handsome young man, to his own great surprise, was so stirred by his emotions that he made his way to the platform to deliver an ardent, powerful, impromptu eulogy to Elijah P. Lovejoy and the causes he had died for. It was the maiden oration of Wendell Phillips, so effective and so moving that it quickly established him as the "golden trumpet" of the abolition movement.

But meanwhile, what of the young slave boy William? When Lovejoy left St. Louis, William was still there, but he was dreaming of escaping north. His first bid for freedom came after a ghastly year spent in the employ of a slave driver. Four times he helped the slave trader take big gangs of slaves south from St. Louis to New Orleans. William's job was caring for the poor creatures, who were handcuffed in pairs and chained in groups of twenty. With their heavy manacles clanking and rattling, the slaves were taken by steamboat from city to city. They had little food and no sanitary facilities, and William found it hard to keep their area of the deck clean.

At St. Louis, Natchez, New Orleans, and other cities along the river the slaves were taken ashore and herded into slave pens for several days while prospective buyers looked them over. At these times William assisted his master in fixing up the appearance of the slaves, cutting and pulling out gray hairs of old men and women to make them look younger, or blacking their gray locks with shoeblack if there were too many gray hairs to pull. Then he had to set the captives dancing and singing to display their vitality to the white men walking about the pen.

Those slaves not purchased in the pen were taken to public auction, and if not sold there, they were put back in chains and taken by steamboat to the next city. New Orleans was the end of the line. Here the slave-driver disposed of all his wares one way or another and began purchasing a new lot of slaves as he and William made their way northward, back to St. Louis.

During that year William saw enough suffering and inhuman treatment of his fellow slaves, and endured enough beatings of his own, to determine him to escape should he ever have the opportunity. He watched babies torn from their mothers, men bought separately from their grief-stricken wives and children, women forced to become mistresses and prostitutes, men beaten and hung from the rafters to be beaten again, and he watched a slave hunted down and killed by a gang of white men for stealing a piece of meat, the victim's body being left where it fell until the trashman carted it off with other street dirt. What he saw and experienced sickened him and turned him to hating white men, for with the exception of Elijah Lovejoy he had never known a decent one.

Although William himself had never been sold, he had watched his only sister bought by a slave driver and taken South, never to be heard from again. That led him to try to escape one night with his mother. In a stolen skiff he rowed across the Mississippi River to Ohio, where mother and son attempted walking by night and hiding by day. But they were overtaken and returned to their owners in St. Louis. As punishment William's mother was sold into a chain gang. William watched her manacled form taken off to labor and die in some far field.

Sold at last to a new master himself, William found a second chance to escape when he was taken on a journey up the Ohio River. On the first day of January 1834 he performed the task of carrying a trunk ashore, and instead of returning to his master on the riverboat, he melted into the crowd. This time he was more cautious, hiding by day, following the North Star by night, eating only what he could secretly steal, until at last he was driven by fever and desperate cold to seek help of a passerby. He was lucky. The man he appealed to along a lonely highway near Dayton, Ohio, was a Quaker, sympathetic to fugitives. The Quaker took William in, fed him, nursed him, clothed him appropriately for an Ohio winter, and gave him money to continue his journey. In gratitude to the kindness of Friend Wells Brown, William adopted his name.

The fugitive made his way to Lake Erie, originally intending to cross into Canada as soon as the ice was gone, but he found temporary employment and relative safety from slave hunters in Cleveland and decided to stay there. He married a free Negro woman and for several summers worked as steward on a Lake Erie steamer. In that job he was able to help dozens of fugitives cross the lake into Canada by secreting them by ones and twos aboard his boat.

When he moved to Buffalo, New York, in search of winter employment, William Wells Brown settled his family into a community of free Negroes in whom he took an interest. He found opportunity to improve his rudimentary education and became involved in some of the problems confronting free blacks. To combat what he considered excessive drinking among the colored people, Brown formed a temperance society. As its president he gained experience in public speaking and parliamentary procedure. Then, in 1843, he attended an antislavery conference held in Buffalo. At it he met Charles Remond and Frederick Douglass, prominent Negroes who acquainted him with William Lloyd Garrison's radical ideas and opened his eyes to the role a free Negro might play in abolition. Shortly afterward William Wells Brown became an agent for the New York Anti-Slavery Society and began speaking in towns near Buffalo about his experiences.

Great was the value to antislavery societies of a black man who could describe the sufferings of the slaves. But the work was not easy. One of Brown's early lectures took him to Attica, New York, on a cold winter's night. He spoke movingly and well to an interested gathering in the local church. After the applause ended and the audience left, Brown found there were no public accommodations where a colored man might spend the night. He returned to the church with its dead stove and walked about all night in the dark, flapping his arms to keep warm.

On another occasion he faced a large, unfriendly group in East Aurora, New York. As soon as he was introduced, rowdies began stamping and whistling and throwing eggs and dried peas. Brown stood his ground until he was hit in the face by an egg which spattered down his coat front. His anger flared. He stepped down from the platform and stood directly before his audience.

"If you don't want me to speak to you this evening, I won't," he shouted above the uproar. "But I will say this. You are cowards, all of you. If any of you were slaves in the South, you wouldn't have the courage to escape."

To his amazement the hecklers ceased their din, surprised looks on their faces. Brown seized the chance to begin telling of his life as a slave. For an hour and a half he described the things he had done and endured. His listeners were impressed. They clapped enthusiastically, and afterward many came forward to shake his hand.

Audiences were so interested in his experiences that in 1847 he wrote a book about his life. *The Narrative of William Wells Brown, a Fugitive Slave, Written by Himself* was a popular volume. Brown wrote well, in simple compelling style. In years to come he would write a narrative about his European experiences as well as two excellent Negro histories.

In 1849 he was sent as representative of the American Peace Society to a peace congress in Paris. Afterward he went to England where he was welcomed by many noted Englishmen and was able to observe the strides England had made during the decade since that country's great effort to emancipate its crown colonies. While he was still abroad the Fugitive Slave Law of 1850 was passed in America, tightening the controls for returning fugitives to their owners. William Wells Brown was afraid to return to America. After all, he was still a fugitive and a very well-known one now. For four more years he traveled in England and on the continent, delivering over a thousand antislavery lectures, until friends in this country could raise the money to purchase his freedom from his former master.

Thus it was that in 1854 Brown reentered the country a free man. He was still enjoying the taste of the words on his tongue when he visited the Remonds in Salem. He planned now to continue the task he had left five years before by becoming a lecturer for the American Anti-Slavery Society.

To me William Wells Brown was an incredible phenomenon. This man who had been born a slave and treated as a brute for twenty years could now sit on Mrs. Remond's parlor sofa with a cup of tea in his hand, entertaining us with tales of his travels in England. True, he was not the polished speaker and writer Charles Remond was, but that did not deter him from speaking effectively from the platform and in the drawing room, from writing histories and novels.

One evening Mr. Brown, the Remonds, and I were discussing *Uncle Tom's Cabin*. I was interested in knowing how accurately Mrs. Stowe's portrayal fit Mr. Brown's knowledge of what slavery was really like.

"It's all she says, but so much worse," William said heatedly. "A white Northerner, particularly a woman, just can't imagine the utter and complete degradation of the slave. A black slave is nothing. He has no rights, he has no feelings, he's nothing. In the eyes of the Southern white he's not really a human being."

"A lot of people have criticized Mrs. Stowe for making the cruelest person in the book a Northerner," I ventured. "They say she was too softhearted toward her Southern characters."

"Well, I tend to agree with Mrs. Stowe," Mr. Brown said. "I never knew *any* Southern slaveowners so afflicted with their consciences as her Augustine St.

Clare, but I'd take a Southern overseer over a Northern one any day of the week. The cruelest overseer I ever knew was a Northerner named John Colburn. Southerners may hate Negroes and may treat them like dirt or like animals or any way you want to say it, but it's a hatred that's born and bred in them. They inherit it from their fathers and they absorb it from the people around them. It's sort of a natural hatred. But a Northerner's hatred is different. It's acquired, and sometimes it's also involved with something abnormal in his personality, and it's a lot worse. I'm referring now to the Northerners who come South and have to cope with slaves. Simon Legree isn't the meanest Northern overseer I've heard of by a long shot."

"But surely," spoke up Mrs. Remond in her sweet voice, "surely there *are* kind Southerners. Particularly among the women; they can't all be demons with the lash. Particularly those who are religious and are guided by Christian precepts."

"Ah, madam"—Mr. Brown turned to her solemnly —"those who are religious are among the worst. Have you ever heard a passage from the Bible that goes, 'He that knoweth his master's will and doeth it not, shall be beaten with many stripes'? It's the golden rule of those masters and mistresses who are most devoted to churchgoing. My master was a religious man, so I know whereof I speak, though he was mild compared to some. The day he took up religion, things became harder for his slaves. Sunday had been our only free day, the only time we might trap or fish a little, or visit or just sleep. Suddenly we couldn't do those things any more. We were breaking the Sabbath if we tried to hoe a little corn patch of our own. No, we had to start attending church morning and evening so we could be told how to behave by a special preacher who taught us slaves the good word. But worst of all, it's easy to find ample justification for slavery in Bible passages, and slaveowners who are religious will trot out a hundred quotations to support their mean ways."

"Still, the Bible is one of the few comforts slaves have, I guess," Sarah Remond remarked with a sigh.

"Yes, and a viperous one it is, in general," William Wells Brown responded. "I never knew a real Uncle Tom, someone who could use piety as his crutch all the while the most terrible things were happening to him. I do know, though, that if a slave was said to 'have religion,' he brought a better price on the auction block. I can hear the dealer now, pushing some young colored girl forward, saying, 'What am I offered for this woman? She's a good cook, a good washer, an obedient servant. She's got religion!' Do you know what that means to a Southerner, to a buyer?"

William Brown paused to look at each of us before he answered. "It means that she's been taught by a white preacher that she must submit to the treatment she receives from white men and women. She must never strike back. God made her to be a slave and she knows it, and she'll never find fault no matter how hard she's whipped."

The words seared themselves on my heart. It was true, as Mr. Brown said, that even I, black, but a woman and a Northerner, could not truly comprehend the degradation of the slaves. But I could and did feel sick at heart on their behalf.

William Brown's visit provided a chance for Charles Remond to recall his own early experiences with the abolitionists. As he and Mr. Brown reminisced, I learned how Mr. Remond first became acquainted with William Lloyd Garrison back in 1831 when the *Liberator* began publication. Remond had helped Garrison establish the New England Anti-Slavery Society at a time when few Northerners were receptive to radical notions about slavery. Remond had also been with Garrison on that day in October 1835 when the editor was mobbed and dragged through the streets of Boston with a rope about his waist. He might have been killed had the police not provided him refuge in the Leverett Street jail.

Remond had stuck by Garrison through years of turmoil within the abolition movement. Garrison was a militant man, whose interests extended beyond anti-slavery to women's rights, temperance, and many other humanitarian reforms. New York members of the American Anti-Slavery Society thought he was diffusing his energies and weakening the abolition effort by espousing so many other causes. In addition, Garrison bitterly denounced the established churches, hurling invectives at this denomination or that minister through the pages of the *Liberator*. More conservative abolitionists were appalled at such actions. Garrison also decried political action to advance the anti-slavery cause, for he eschewed the Constitution and would not work within its established systems. Other abolitionists felt, however, that by electing the right representatives in Congress and influencing party politics, the emancipation effort would progress. Most of all, Garrison wanted "immediate and unconditional emancipation." The New York group put a more conservative interpretation on the phrase.

The result was that in 1840 the American Anti-Slavery Society with Garrison at its helm split off from the politically-minded group which had joined interests with the newly evolving Liberty party. Garrison went his own way, carrying on an independent, moral, highly radical campaign.

The spring that these internal fractures were occurring, a World Anti-Slavery Conference was called in London. Garrison, Wendell Phillips, and Charles Remond went as delegates. So did several women, including Lydia Maria Child and the liberal Friend, Lucretia Mott. Garrison had long championed the rights of women, and one of the causes of the split within the American Anti-Slavery Society had been his attempt to include women on the executive committee. But women by tradition and by law had been kept in the background. A number of American women were beginning to protest their rights and were being heard. But in 1840 a woman had few rights, being legally subject to her father or husband. By tradition she belonged at home, tending to child rearing and housekeeping. She had little chance for a good education, and while she might have ideas or opinions, she had better express them privately. In public, women were seen but not heard. There was strong feeling in this country and in Europe that women surely should not participate in the World Anti-Slavery Conference.

When the meetings began in London, Wendell Phillips was the only male American delegate present, for Garrison and Remond had been delayed en route. The American women had been left out of the program and refused seats on the floor. Phillips arose in the convention to plead on their behalf, but to no avail. The ladies were assigned to the gallery with the onlookers. When Garrison arrived, he was angry. If the women delegates could not be admitted, then neither would he be. With a great show of indignation he relinquished his own seat and joined Mrs. Mott and the other women in the balcony, where the bald head of America's most prominent abolitionist was very conspicuous among the ladies' bonnets. Charles Remond followed him to the gallery.

In talking of the London conference, Mr. Remond could still summon great feeling to his description of what took place. Almost fifteen years afterward, driving with me one day along Salem's sea road, he was full of anger and mortification at the memory of his voyage to England. The only Negro among the delegates, he had been forced by the captain of his ship to go into special accommodations reserved for colored people. He had had to sleep and eat his meals in segregated, uncomfortable compartments throughout the rough voyage.

"I learned two things from that journey, Charlotte," Mr. Remond told me that autumn afternoon as we drove past the bay, calm, beautiful, capped by a light haze and bedecked with one or two sails upon its bosom. "Actually I knew both things already. That trip just confirmed my thinking. One was that the handmaiden of slavery in this country is prejudice. It's a hydra-headed monster that pops up in every conceivable form in every state in the Union, and you won't begin to lick it until slavery's gone, the way it is in England. The other thing I learned was that women are practically as enslaved as black men, and if I believe in freedom for my race, I am as much committed to freedom for every underprivileged individual, black or white, male or female. You can't entirely separate these issues. I wasn't really in sympathy with women making a public commotion about their rights to property and money and children, or about them wanting to enter men's professions, but at the London Conference I had a taste of what they're up against. They have a hard row to hoe, too."

"Did you know I have a bloomer costume, Mr. Remond?" I asked playfully. "I wore it to climb your cherry tree a few weeks ago to pick the cherries for Mrs. Remond."

Charles Remond laughed. The outfit to which I referred was considered scandalous by many. It had been designed by a feminist named Amelia Bloomer, who protested that women were too weighted down by long cumbersome skirts. Her notion of freedom was a tunic worn over a short skirt and long pantaloons, thereafter called bloomers, which fastened at the ankles. The costume had become a symbol of revolt against restrictions on women. My bloomer garb was navy-blue serge, and now that I was used to the odd feeling it gave my legs, I liked it considerably, although I would never have had nerve to wear it in public.

"If you're such an ardent feminist as all that, Charlotte, I guess you'd better take the reins" was Mr. Remond's dry comment. So saying, he handed them over to me, knowing how I delighted to guide the trotting horses along the scenic roads surrounding Salem.

Yet Charles Remond had many happy memories, too, of that trip to England in 1840. It had been far from unpleasurable. He was well received by the Britishers and became a very popular lecturer. He spoke well, as I knew, and was invited to do so throughout England and Ireland. In the latter country sixty thousand Irishmen signed a petition calling for emancipation of the American Negro, a document Charles Remond bore home proudly to unroll before a crowd in Faneuil Hall. He discovered that his fame and popularity in the United States had increased immeasurably because of his success abroad. In fact, he found himself the most prominent free Negro in the abolition movement.

Charles Remond enjoyed the memory of his triumph. He was much sought after as a speaker, and he found antislavery audiences looking to him for advice and guidance. I knew, however, from what my father had told me of Mr. Remond, that his singular prominence was short-lived. A while later a new star appeared on the horizon, one whose brilliance muted the performance of Charles Remond. At an antislavery meeting on Nantucket Island in the summer of 1841, a strong, handsome black man with deep eyes, a vibrant voice, and an astonishing head of bushy black hair unexpectedly rose in the audience to tell the gathering of his experiences as an escaped slave. The man was Frederick Douglass. Abolitionists took note of his commanding presence, his natural talent for speaking and his obvious concern for his fellow man, and quickly adopted him into the movement. Frederick Douglass shortly became an outstanding leader of the Massachusetts and New England Anti-Slavery societies, and before long much of the attention that had been Charles Remond's was focused on Frederick Douglass, whose abilities as a platform orator and as a prolific writer surpassed Remond's own. Douglass was encouraged to write *The Narrative of the Life of Frederick Douglass.* It was a lucid, well-written book that appeared in 1845, when its author was about twenty-seven. I read it and reread it as a child, and knew that Frederick Douglass described not just the miseries of his own early life, but of three million enslaved blacks.

Like William Wells Brown, Douglass was the child of a slave woman and a white man, but he had been taken from his mother as an infant, and since she died of overwork in the fields when he was small, he never learned who his father was. Douglass grew up on a large prosperous plantation in Maryland, slave of an overseer so cruel that one of Douglass' early memories was of seeing his aunt hung by her wrists from a hook in the ceiling and lashed with a cowhide until both blood and screams came from her.

Frederick's early years were spent under one mean

overseer after another. His descriptions of the barba-
rous treatment of Negro slaves made the slavers in
Mrs. Stowe's novel seem kindly by comparison. Douglass was sent to Baltimore to live for seven years with
relatives of his owner, his new master being a tolerable
human being and his mistress kind enough that she
taught him to read and write. When Frederick later
returned to the plantation fields, he was considered
spoiled by the relative freedom and privileges of city
life. The brutal field labor and violent punishments
meted out by an evil-tempered, whip-wielding overseer caused Frederick to become rebellious. One day
he struck back at his overseer, a rare event, for such reaction was pretext enough to kill a slave. But Frederick survived the incident and was hired out to a kinder
master, though thereafter he was determined to escape
from slavery.

Jailed for a while after an abortive attempt at escape, Frederick was again sent to Baltimore and hired
out to a shipbuilder. While learning that trade he was
nearly killed in a fight between black and white apprentice carpenters, but again he survived and became
a skilled caulker, able to earn a few pennies of his own.
Watching his opportunity carefully, Douglass at last
escaped via ship to New York. For years he would not
tell how he had accomplished the feat or who had
helped him, for fear of reprisal.

Frederick Douglass was an attractive, intelligent
man who confirmed the views of New England abolitionists. On the subject of religion, for instance, the
topic on which Garrison had taken so vociferous a

stand, Douglass stated unequivocally, "The religion of the South is a mere covering for the most horrid crimes—a justifier of the most appalling barbarity—a sanctifier of the most hateful frauds—and a dark shelter under which the darkest, foulest, grossest, and most infernal deeds of slaveholders find the strongest protection. Were I to be again reduced to the chains of slavery, next to that enslavement I should regard being the slave of a religious master the greatest calamity that could befall me."

Since the Frederick Douglass narrative was in my grandfather's library, I had early absorbed the author's opinions into my own thinking. Much of what I read and indeed saw for myself confirmed the view that the Christian church in America bore great responsibility for supporting the status quo, for being uninterested in reform. Congregational churches in New England had banned abolitionists from their pulpits. Most white churches in the country refused to admit Negroes or else assigned them to segregated pews. It was only in the larger cities, principally in the Boston area, that the Theodore Parkers and Thomas Wentworth Higginsons lashed out from the pulpit against slavery.

The religious aspect of the antislavery cause deeply concerned Mary Shepard, my teacher at Salem's Higginson Grammar School. Within a few days of my entering the school she proffered friendship, and my friend she became and remained for many years. We first spoke about abolition one early summer afternoon when classes were over and, in order to become better acquainted with me, she had asked me to stay to help arrange some papers. I discovered at once that she was a kindred spirit in her opposition to slavery, but that as a devout Christian she was troubled by the anti-Christian nature of the movement.

"From what I've observed, Charlotte," she stated firmly, "from what I know, I should say, I just don't believe that ministers and the church in general promote slavery. You can enter any meetinghouse in Salem, or almost any town round about, and hear slavery called wicked and an infamous system."

"Of course, I haven't been here long enough to know," was my reply. "I hope what you say is true. But at home, in Philadelphia, such things aren't talked about in church. The congregations wouldn't stand for it. And how better do you support an evil than by keeping silent about its existence?"

"One bad apple doesn't spoil the barrel," Mary Shepard pointed out lightly. "The whole Christian religion can't be condemned for what a few of its churches do."

"No," I assented. "But Mr. Barnes, who is pastor of the First Presbyterian Church of Philadelphia, says that in America the church is the bulwark of slavery. He claims that the clergy by their neutralism and lack of concern buoy up the system."

"I'm glad to hear that you attend, my dear, and are attentive." Miss Shepard smiled at me. "Here. Please take these erasers outside and beat the chalk out of them. Against the steps will do."

Outdoors the sky was blue, the sun warm, and a gentle breeze stirred the new, still undersized leaves of the maples in front of the grammar school. I pounded the erasers briskly and watched the dry, white powder sift onto the grass. When I reentered the schoolroom, wiping chalk dust off my hands and frock, Miss Shepard looked very solemn.

"Charlotte, tell me. This is an odd question to be asking when we scarcely know each other, but are you a Christian?"

I knew she wondered whether I had formally professed my faith and joined the church. I had not, and told her so. I told her, too, because she was the kind of person to whom you opened your heart, that I despaired of ever becoming a Christian.

"I think such dark thoughts, Miss Shepard," I confessed. "I know it's wrong, but I hate the people who hate me and who hate black people. How can I love my enemy? I've tried to do it, but I don't and I can't forgive the people who oppress my race."

"Perhaps it's the oppression and not the oppressors you must learn to hate, Charlotte," Miss Shepard suggested gently.

"It's so hard to separate the two. If you just knew the thousand tiny ways in which one can be made to feel despised and unwanted! When a girl who's been friendly in the classroom snubs me on the street, I can't separate the action from the actor. When I'm told the tickets in my hand won't let me into the museum, it's hard to hate the regulations and not the doorman too. Sometimes I am truly amazed that we colored manage to go on living sanely, that we're not all misanthropes!"

"Well, you, at least, are not one yet, my dear girl," laughed Miss Shepard, giving me a quick hug. "What do you say to a brisk walk this lovely afternoon to get the cobwebs out of our lungs. Things look quite ship-shape here." She stacked some papers and neatly anchored them with *Familiar Lectures on Botany*.

"Have you visited Harmony Grove yet, Charlotte?" she continued, taking my arm and steering me out the door. "It's the most beautiful cemetery in the world. Later this summer the whole class will spend a day there identifying trees. It's been planted as an arboretum, and you'll find every variety of New England tree, not to mention bird, along the promenades."

So ended our serious interview, the first of many, many talks we would have together on this subject and a hundred others, for I felt more at ease with Mary Shepard than with any other white person I have known. With her I could discuss the issues that alienated our races, and though we did not always agree, I could count on her understanding of my special problems. Mary Shepard was one of those rare creatures whose warmth, kindness, and innate sensitivity drew out the shyest and made them feel wanted. She offered me and so many others not merely sympathy but understanding and intelligent friendship. Later, when I came to know her better, I learned she had known deep sorrow during her young life, and in Harmony Grove rested several who had been nearest and dearest to her. Her concern with the religious state of her friends was a natural and an abiding one.

One of the very special people whom Mary Shepard

was able to woo from seclusion was Elizabeth Hawthorne, sister of the author, Nathaniel Hawthorne.
Miss Shepard induced Miss Hawthorne to accompany
our class on occasional outings, else I would never
have known her, for she lived a lonely, retired life in
lodgings on a farm in Beverly. It was exciting to me
to realize that Elizabeth Hawthorne had grown up
in that dark, gloomy Salem house that Nathaniel had
recently made famous in *The House of the Seven
Gables*. The day Miss Hawthorne accompanied us to
Marblehead beach, I sat near her among the recesses
in the huge rocks to watch the waves come dashing in,
breaking with great fury and sending spray high onto
our shoes and skirts.

I spoke of my admiration for her brother, and Miss
Hawthorne opened her locket to show me his portrait
—a splendid head with noble brow and dark expres-
sive eyes. She told me many interesting things about
him, that he had always called their home "Castle Dismal" because it was so dreary and musty inside, that
Nathaniel and his two sisters had been brought up
amidst an overwhelming sense of the past, sponsored
partly by their beautiful but reclusive mother and
partly by the old furniture and portraits and family
tales with which they shared the house.

Nathaniel was happily married now, and his life
much sunnier, his writing going well. Miss Hawthorne
made me wince, though, by mentioning her brother's
scorn for the horde of "scribbling women" who tried
to write books. I winced still harder to hear that he
had once thrown away his little daughter's notebook

and pen when he discovered her trying to write a story. Evidently he was permitting the same child's talents with the paintbrush to develop naturally, which I suppose somewhat compensated for such ruthlessness.

We wandered up and down the beach at low tide that day, gathering the smooth, glistening, sea-hewn stones and all manner of oddly shaped seaweed. Miss Hawthorne gave me a white pebble struck through with tints of red-orange to remember her by—as if I could forget. We stayed to watch a glorious sunset, a sailor's delight, then directed the carriages homeward in the deepening twilight.

During the time I spent in New England, a period covering four years, I came to love and accept it as my home. In its atmosphere I could breathe more freely, along the streets of its cities and towns I could walk with more dignity, than elsewhere. Philadelphia with its proscriptions and seething hatred toward the Negro would never again be natural to me. Salem itself I grew to love in the easy, effortless way one comes to love a child. Suddenly it was familiar, part of me, and I could not imagine existing so happily elsewhere. I loved an old-fashioned quality about the town, the way it focused seaward and the way its residential streets ran steeply uphill, perpendicular to the water.

Salem was one of the earliest settlements on the New England coast. For years now gone by, it had been a major commercial port for whaling ships and East India merchants. The beautiful homes of wealthy sea captains lined lovely, elm-shaded Chestnut and Lafayette Streets, giving Salem its unique, aristocratic air.

I often strolled the nearly patterned brick sidewalks, glancing through imposing fences at beautiful gardens. Salem was still a prosperous community. The main business street, paralleling the wharves, featured commerce aplenty, with the customs house and the railroad station principal centers of activity. Then came neighborhoods of pretty, irregularly distanced white houses with green blinds and little gardens behind neat palings. Short side streets led to the wharves and the water. Down one, occupied by a cotton factory, you came to a miniature beach with a long, projecting rocky point. Here I often sat on hot days to look at the bay and the water.

The town was surrounded by high hills called the Pastures, which commanded lovely views and provided me many delightful rambles. On Gallows Hill, Salem's witches had been hung two centuries before. On all grew violets and anemones in springtime and myriad other wildflowers in summer.

I made a few close friends in Salem: the Remonds, of course, and Mary Shepard, and also the Israel Putnams, a Negro family who kept a notions store and were very active in antislavery. At school I had a bosom friend, Lizzie Church, a white student from Nova Scotia, who was very bright and who shared my own interest in literature and languages. Together we read aloud *The Genius of Scotland* and Macaulay's *History of England* and other books we could find about the British Isles. Since Lizzie and I were especially close to our teacher, often visiting her at her lodgings to talk and share her books, and even occasionally glimpsing portions of the fascinating journal she kept, we were looked upon with some envy by our classmates. To be envied was a rare treat for me, and I can't say I didn't enjoy it.

Lizzie and I also had in common the desire to become teachers. The Salem Normal School had recently opened its doors, tuition free, to young ladies who would agree to teach for a period in the Massachusetts public schools. Its square, massive edifice, irreverently called "the soapbox," beckoned me from the corner opposite Higginson Grammar School. At the end of a year's work in the grammar school I took the normal-school examinations and was accepted. Indeed, a more difficult hurdle was to convince Father that I should stay on in Salem. He wanted me to come home, partly because he missed me but also because his business affairs were not going well and he could not send much money for my support. Both Miss Shepard and Mr. Edwards, principal of the normal school, wrote Father of how well my studies were going and how good my prospects were of obtaining a teaching position once I completed them, and he finally assented to my staying.

So it was that in June of 1856, after a year's training at the normal school, the conservative city of Salem for the first time offered a situation as public school teacher to one of my race! I became assistant at the Epes Grammar School, receiving a salary of two hundred dollars a year, for which I worked very hard and at times despondently. For the truth is, I found the role of student far preferable and easier than that of teacher. I tried at first to combine the two, continuing with my precious French and German lessons in addition to preparing the lessons for my all-too-unruly scholars. The result was that I exhausted myself, in fact verged on being ill, until I decided to give up my languages and concentrate on teaching alone. All my dreams of learning, of writing, of becoming an antislavery speaker in addition to earning a living, must wait.

Tired and discouraged as at times I might be in Salem, life there was never dull. There was always something going on, some meeting or lecture or event to look forward to, some new, exciting person to meet. Sooner or later all the great and near great came to Salem, if for no other reason than to speak before the Salem Lyceum.

Many New England towns had lyceums for learning about the most stimulating topics of the day. Few, however, were as enterprising as the Salem Lyceum. The idea of having prominent ministers, scholars, and political leaders come before a meeting to inform and enlighten had caught the public fancy. The urge to learn was in the air, and people wanted to hear views on every subject from women's rights to new archaeological discoveries in Greece. A great assortment of such facts and opinions and theories were served up in the Salem Lyceum. So popular was the lyceum lecture series, in fact, that before long there were two series, and since abolitionist speakers were not included in ei-

ther of them, the hall was made available to the Salem
Female Anti-Slavery Society for a series of antislavery
talks.

Many and many an evening I eagerly approached
the doors of the big, square neoclassical building that
housed the Salem Lyceum. The hall seated seven hundred people in tiers that rose in great semicircles facing the speaker's platform. Before us, on the rostrum,
might appear the handsome figure of Harvard nat-
uralist Louis Agassiz preparing to enlighten us on
"The Animal Kingdom." Or the eminent Congregational minister from Brooklyn, Henry Ward Beecher,
might be ready to address us in his simple, earnest
manner on "Patriotism," advancing along the way sin-
cere arguments for giving women the right to vote.
Or the attractive but oddly mannered Concord phi-
losopher, Ralph Waldo Emerson, might send his
polished thoughts on "Beauty" or "Works and Days"
flying past our ears. The times encouraged outstanding rhetoric, and there was no lack of great orators in
our corner of New England.

Only rarely was the audience disappointed in a
speaker. Most could stimulate the finer sensibilities of
their listeners, could arouse the nobler passions, by
giving voice to inspiring ideas in an eloquent manner.
After the best lectures I would float home, ballooned
up by lofty optimism in the innate moral goodness of
human nature, supported somewhere above real earth
by feelings of faith in man's perfectibility, to confide
the haunting messages of the speaker to my journal.

Yet no speakers surpassed the abolitionists, in my

opinion. Give a man a soul-searing crusade like anti-slavery, and he could outdo the most impassioned defender of medieval chivalry and the best-informed eulogizer of "Ecuador's Cultural Heritage."

The most stirring antislavery lecture I heard in Salem brought out such crowds that, arriving at Lyceum Hall unexpectedly late, the Remonds and I could not find seats. We stood to hear one of the few women who dared raise her voice in public. She was Lucy Stone, a small, dainty young lady, a little prim and not particularly pretty. That she should have become notorious for her opinions about slavery and about the rights of women seemed surprising. Yet she had vowed never to marry because with marriage a woman surrendered legal control of herself to her husband. Six months after her appearance in Salem she did marry, but to a man who respected her opinions. As part of their marriage vows Lucy and her husband read a protest against the laws that denied a woman control of her person, property, and children. And the Reverend Thomas Wentworth Higginson, who performed the ceremony, agreed to omit the word "obey" from the wedding service.

The night I heard her in Salem, Lucy Stone appeared in bloomer costume to launch her attack on slavery. Her lecture was earnest and impressive, some parts of it very beautiful. It was an appeal to the noblest and warmest sympathies of our nature on behalf of the oppressed. Looking around the crowded hall, I saw many among the large, attentive audience who had probably never attended an antislavery lecture before. While undoubtedly they had come more to stare than to listen, I hoped Lucy Stone's touching appeal might yet reach them. "From noble thoughts spring noble words and deeds," I reminded myself as applause rose loudly to the lyceum ceiling, where in decorative tints Apollo in his chariot ushered in the morn.

Of all the noted people I had the privilege of hearing and meeting and knowing in Salem, the friendship I prize above all others is that with the gentle Quaker poet, John Greenleaf Whittier. Inspired by reading some of his verses, one day I boldly sent a letter to his home in Amesbury. Years before, I reminded him, when he lived in Philadelphia editing an antislavery newspaper, Mr. Whittier had been a good friend of James Forten's and a frequent guest in the house where I later grew up. Now I wanted him to know that I too admired his poetry, so much of it devoted to denouncing slavery, and I thanked him for using his great talents on behalf of my race.

To my utter joy I received a reply from him and not long afterward a visit. When Sarah Remond in great excitement summoned me downstairs to meet the unexpected caller, I was rendered almost speechless with surprise. In fact Sarah—whom speech never failed—supplied most of the conversation during the short visit. I was at first somewhat shocked by Mr. Whittier's appearance. My grandmother and aunts had often described the tall, handsome young man who had frequented our home twenty-five years earlier. He had had brilliant eyes and a fine head covered with dark, curly hair. Still tall and erect of carriage, the man I saw was thin and pale, his sparse locks streaked with gray, his face bearing the imprint of bad health. Yet there was still fire in his eyes, and his smile was the sweetest I have ever seen on any man's face.

We talked on that occasion of the differences between New England and Philadelphia, and the poet told me a lot about the agricultural life of the region. He had grown up on a New Hampshire farm and knew well the hardships of that life. I took him to see Miss Shepard, as ardent an admirer of Whittier as myself, and when he left, he extended an invitation to us both to visit his home on the Merrimack River.

In the next few years Mary Shepard and I visited him not once but several times. And even after I left Salem and became involved in other adventures, Mr. Whittier and I exchanged letters and visits for long years. He lived simply and quietly with his lovely, shy sister, Elizabeth, in an Amesbury cottage that in summertime was filled with flowers and sunshine, and always with that pervading peace that was the Quaker spirit. Although he was known to be shy in public, at home among friends John Greenleaf Whittier was warm and genial. He had a boyish frankness of manner, a natural love of fun, and keen appreciation for the humorous in life. Assisted by bright, childlike comments from his sister, he would tell delightful stories about the "lion-hunters"—mostly ladies—who traced him to his lair and made a great to-do over his poetry. We talked freely about many, many topics, including marriage. As a bachelor, I told him, he was ineligible to opine so freely about the problems of that estate. On occasion he took us rowing upon the Merrimack, and once in springtime rowed me up a pretty little creek, the Artichoke, where flowers bloomed profusely along the banks and the scent of blossoms was sweetly overpowering.

Sweet and idyllic as these memories of New England are, they do not represent the true temper of my inner feelings or of the times in general. It was actually a seething, boiling period, those years before the Civil War. Within I coped as best I could with my own frustrations of meeting kindness and consideration here, hatred and cold prejudice there. One day I might be escorted to the home of the venerable Theodore Parker, that great and kindly preacher who called himself the most hated man in New England, for he was aware of the enmity his radical religious beliefs had stirred. So worn by zest for overwork was Parker that he looked far older than his forty-five years. When we rang his doorbell, he greeted us cordially and showed me through his vast library. The books, fifteen thousand volumes, swarmed all the walls of the three-story house, and still he bought and devoured more.

Another day I might attend the Annual Anti-Slavery Bazaar, held each Christmastime in Boston, to be greeted most kindly to right and left by Mr. Wendell Phillips, Mr. Garrison, and Mrs. Lydia Maria Child. There also I might have the honor and pleasure of walking arm in arm through the fair with Maria Weston Chapman, that loveliest, bravest, and most determined of antislavery ladies, who had organized the whole festive display.

But then on other days my heart bled at the futility of a few white kindnesses meted out to me among the gross indignities handed most free Negroes and the abuse delivered slaves. Each Fourth of July those fools of patriots who celebrated their mockery called Independence sickened my soul. And at our nation's capital political gains were being made by men who would exploit the black man and spread the stain of slavery farther westward and northward across America.

Early in the spring of 1856 the United States senator from Massachusetts, Charles Sumner, an outspoken advocate of human rights and abolition, delivered a speech in Congress concerning the "crime against Kansas." It was a scholarly but highly abusive speech, especially to Southern ears, and it so enraged a representative from South Carolina that next day he entered the Senate chamber and attacked Sumner with a cane. The attack was sudden and so vicious that Sumner, pinned at his desk, was very badly injured. It was several years before he fully recovered from the damage to his spine.

The "crime against Kansas" was this. In 1854, just as I came to Salem, a bill had been passed by Congress that voided the Missouri Compromise of 1820, that old agreement which had drawn a firm line between slave and free states at the thirty-sixth parallel. The new Kansas-Nebraska Bill made Northerners—Free-Soilers, in particular—hopping mad because it ignored the old boundary and declared that the settlers of the Kansas and Nebraska territories should decide for themselves whether to be slave or free. Popular sovereignty, the new plan was called, and the vote was to be taken once the sparsely settled areas were filled with enough citizens to make them eligible for statehood.

The race was on. Whether Kansas and Nebraska went slave or free would be determined by who got there first, Northern settlers or Southern. Almost lost in the commotion was the calm, clear logic of an obscure, lanky Illinois politician named Abraham Lincoln who, in a series of debates with the originator of the Kansas-Nebraska Bill, Stephen Douglas, argued that the right to determine the fate of future states belonged to all the citizens of the United States, not just those who lived in the disputed territory.

But Lincoln's words went unheeded. In Massachusetts and elsewhere in New England, emigrant aid societies sprang up to outfit hardy pioneers willing to stake three-year claims in Kansas. Meanwhile, from the South, particularly Missouri, just as many Southerners crossed the border to settle the broad, dry plains. Some planned to settle only temporarily, until they could influence a proslavery vote, after which they would return to richer Missouri farms. In addition, some determined Missourians known as border ruffians armed themselves to harass Northern settlers and to try to prevent them entering Kansas at all.

The border ruffians made life extremely unpleasant for free-state settlers. They conducted a perpetual desultory guerrilla warfare against the immigrants, some of whom spread out to settle individual farms in the far-flung prairies and some of whom grouped together to establish such towns as Topeka and Lawrence, Kansas. Not only did the ruffians harass the settlers by burning crops and killing cattle, they formed an informal militia, backed by proslavery officials who temporarily gained the governmental hand in Kansas, and attacked Lawrence, sacking the town and killing several settlers. It was this act that provoked Sumner's "crime against Kansas" speech.

Retaliation by the free-state settlers was swift. A few nights after the razing of Lawrence, a band of seven men massacred five proslavery settlers on Pottawatomie Creek. Leader of the band was John Brown, of whom the country would shortly hear more. Such modified but fierce warfare continued for several years and made the settling of Kansas a real challenge to the North.

Later, during the Civil War, when I came to know the Worcester minister and antislavery agitator Thomas Wentworth Higginson, he told me of his experiences during these troubled times. He himself made two excursions into Kansas the summer and autumn of 1856. The first time he assessed the needs and route for a New England expedition, for by then the border ruffians had closed the Missouri River, chief route into the new territory. On his second trip, for the National Kansas Aid Committee, Higginson escorted a party from the last civilized outpost at Iowa City along the new alternative, a long, dangerous journey across six hundred miles of Iowa and Nebraska prairie into Kansas.

As soon as Higginson entered Nebraska, the law was in his own hands, and his experiences accompanying and protecting twenty-eight wagons with some two hundred men, women, and children through lawless lands were full of incident. Desolate landscape and fear of attack by proslavery bands were headaches, but most discouraging was the sight of tired, despondent, defeated families straggling back out of Kansas. In spite of it all, the settlers held high hopes. They were well armed and well equipped, and their great determination eventually won the day. In the summer of 1859 Kansas adopted a constitution prohibiting slavery, and two years later was admitted to the Union.

But the proslavery forces knew other victories. A great blow to Northerners was the 1857 Dred Scott decision, a Supreme Court case involving the rights of a slave who had been taken by his master into a free state and then carried back into slavery. In a highly disputed decision, Chief Justice Taney declared that Dred Scott not only had no right to his freedom, but that no Negroes had any rights that need be respected by white men. The Negro was not a citizen, and the Declaration of Independence did not apply to him. It was a terrible blow to my race and all who supported us.

These were radical times, when feelings between North and South were raw and agitated, and when certain men were not afraid to speak out and to take action against the things they judged immoral and wrong. Perhaps the man who seemed the epitome of moral righteousness, the Puritan spirit incarnate, was the tall, spare homespun figure of John Brown. He was a farmer, but looked and talked and acted like a prophet. His burning eyes, flowing white hair and beard, commanded attention. The Bible was his source of inspiration, and he believed that his life was a God-directed mission to free the enslaved. He was a fanatic, yet he did not strike reasonable men as mad.

When John Brown secretly approached a small group of influential abolitionists with a plan for large-scale harboring of fugitives in the Allegheny Mountains, there to form a free colony or else a temporary refuge for slaves fleeing on to Canada, the abolitionists thought the idea plausible. They agreed to give money and arms to John Brown. Wealthy Gerrit Smith of New York State, noted Dr. Samuel Gridley Howe of Boston, and radical Rev. Thomas Wentworth Higginson of Worcester were members of the small group that worked in his behalf.

John Brown's plans grew and changed over a considerable period of time. How much was known among his supporters about the changes has never been entirely clear. The fact is that finally, on the night of October 16, 1858, John Brown's long months of plotting and scheming on behalf of the slave evolved into an act of treason against the United States Government. Using a supply of Sharp's rifles that Higginson had originally escorted west for the Kansas Aid Society, Brown and a band of twenty-two men stole into Harpers Ferry, Virginia, took some white citizens hostage, and freed their slaves. But the slaves in the neighborhood did not join Brown in insurrection as Brown expected they would, and instead of causing a great uprising, Brown quickly found himself and his men barricaded in the armory with federal troops marching down upon them. Within two days John Brown and such of his band who hadn't escaped or been killed were captured. Within a few weeks they were tried and hung.

John Brown rejected any efforts among his many supporters to save him from the gallows. He realized his death would make him a martyr to the cause of freedom for the slave and that he would accomplish more by dying than he could by continuing to live.

"I pity the poor in bondage that have none to help them," he stated with deep calm before his trial. "That is why I am here; not to gratify any personal animosity, revenge or vindictive spirit. It is my sympathy with the oppressed and wronged, that are as good as you and as precious in the sight of God. . . . You may dispose of me easily, but the question is still to be settled—this Negro question—the end of that is not yet."

Just a year and a half later, many thousands of Northern men may have recalled Brown's words while tramping off to war to the strains of "John Brown's body lies a-mouldering in the grave, His soul goes marching on."

By the time of John Brown's raid on Harpers Ferry and the ensuing excitement it stirred in New England,

I was no longer in Salem, but was living again in the city of my birth. In my personal life several sad and difficult events had taken place. The first was the death of my beloved second mother, Amy Matilda Remond, in the summer of 1856. Her going left a great void in the lives of all in that household on Dean Street, for her kindness, thoughtfulness, and industry had held our world together, and once she was gone we began to spin apart.

Mr. Remond, who had always been a model of gentlemanliness and courtesy, took his wife's death extremely hard. He became despondent, moody, and increasingly irritable, until Sarah and I came to welcome his periods of travel and dread the times he was at home. Those with whom he worked were dismayed by the change in him, for he began to indulge in petty grievances and jealousies. His envy of Frederick Douglass became outspoken, and perhaps was encouraged by the fact that Douglass and Garrison had recently broken over Douglass' growing interest in politics. Whatever the causes, within a year of Mrs. Remond's death I made arrangements to leave the Remond home and board with my friends, the Putnams. It was a far less favorable arrangement because their house was small and crowded.

But, in addition, I was not well. My teaching was interrupted twice by spells of lung fever, and in between I was constantly tired and on the verge of collapse. Finally, in March of 1858, I said farewell to Salem and the few dear friends I had there and boarded the cars for New York and Philadelphia. I felt that in the four years of my New England sojourn I had both aged and matured. I was hardly returning to Pennsylvania a triumphant, conquering hero, for so few of my dreams and ambitions for leading an active and earnest life had been realized, and I knew not what I would do next. But when health returned, I told myself, so would hope, and to that I looked forward.

Chapter 4

~~~~~~

Sometimes I think that if a sponge quietly erased the events of the next four years in my life, I would never miss them and nobody would be the wiser. They were troubled years for me and for the nation. It was a period in which I drifted, unsure of myself, unhappy and prey to bouts of illness and depression, not knowing what direction my life was taking. The direction of national events, on the other hand, was all too plain. As currents in a stream converge with increasing force and swiftness in a narrowing passage, political events and sectional feelings moved strongly and inexorably toward war.

I kept my journal only sketchily between 1858 and 1862, sometimes neglecting it for months altogether, then in a fit of remorse, frantically filling page after page in a futile attempt to recapture events fled by. I was twenty-one the summer after I left Salem, a slim young woman of olive-brown complexion not unattractive in appearance. Though I was not beautiful, or really even pretty, if my mirror did not lie I had a look of fine-boned intelligence that adequately compensated for such deficiencies. Of an age when any girl's thoughts and longings occasionally turn to love and marriage, mine frequently did so, though for no particular reason and with no particular person in mind. There were times when I ached to find another human being to share my most private thoughts, to care for me and about me, to hold my hand and possess my heart while I in turn could hold and possess his. Such were my dreams, and dreams they remained, for I met no one who eased the sense of longing in my life.

While growing up, I had always assumed that by the time I was twenty-one I would be bride and wife, but I found myself instead at that august age quite alone and unattached, with no prospect of altering the situation. I had assumed two other things as well: first, that I should have found the opportunity to travel abroad, to see the many places that called so enticingly from the books I read; and second, that I should have thrown myself passionately into some cause to aid humanity. That neither of these visions approached reality was further cause of that depressed condition that clung to me for several months after returning to Philadelphia.

It was difficult to adjust to being back in Pennsylvania, not only because of the more proscriptive attitude toward black people, but because I had grown used to a rural setting. Sitting on a bench in Independence Square, I would turn my back to the noisy street, the shoulder-to-shoulder shops, the steady flow of people, and the carts and carriages rumbling over cobblestones. Riveting my attention instead upon the trees, grass, and few frisking squirrels, I would try unsuccessfully to wish the city away. But always it would intrude with its cries and its clamor. How few pleasant, happy faces one saw in the city, I mused. How many sad and careworn ones! They quite reflected my own inner feelings.

The first weeks back at Lombard Street I spent resting and reacquiring my normal strength. Everyone indulged me, permitting me only the lightest household tasks and letting me spend whole mornings leafing through books, or afternoons visiting art galleries to feast my eyes and sensibilities on the romantic, sentimental oils and engravings so much in vogue. I read a great deal, everything from the newspapers to the latest antislavery tracts and current novels. I even got out Grandfather's papers and letters, and perused them with leisurely interest. What insight they provided into dear Grandfather's venerable character, and how unworthy they made me feel to be his offspring.

Days when I was feeling more ambitious I would go calling with aunts Sarah and Margaretta or attend the meetings of the Philadelphia Female Anti-Slavery Society. I also formed the habit of stopping in every week or so at the Philadelphia antislavery office on

North Fifth Street. There I could catch up on the latest publications and news, or perhaps cross paths with some interesting visitor whose concern for abolition drew him to those upstairs rooms that served as the vital center of antislavery activities in the city.

During a week I knew Charles Sumner to be in town, I might climb the stairs to the antislavery office two or three times, spurred by the hope of shaking hands with the great senator who had suffered so severely for his views on slavery and the Kansas-Nebraska Bill. Even more pleasant, though, were the days I found no one there but William Still, clerk of the society and one of the kindest, bravest black men alive. He seemed always to have leisure for visitors, and over a period of months I came to know him quite well, in fact, to count him my friend. Father and Uncle Robert Purvis admired Mr. Still, and also depended upon him greatly, for he was a key link in Vigilance Committee activities. He was not shy in talking about himself, of his childhood and how he had been drawn into the center of antislavery doings. In response to my many questions during afternoon visits, I learned a lot about his life.

William Still had been born in the New Jersey pine barrens, youngest of the numerous children of Levin and Charity Still. His father was a former Maryland slave who had purchased his freedom. His mother succeeded on her second attempt in escaping from slavery, bringing two small children with her and leaving two young sons behind in bondage. William and several brothers and sisters were born in the North. Steel, rather than Still, was the family's original name, but Levin and Charity felt obliged to disguise it for protection against Charity's recapture.

Growing up, William worked with his brothers and sisters on the forty-acre farm his parents managed to procure by hard, unceasing labor. The family was poor, and William had few educational opportunities. At the age of twenty he left home looking for work and soon settled in Philadelphia. There he became attracted to the Pennsylvania Society for the Abolition of Slavery, and he flung himself into its activities, becoming increasingly involved in helping fugitive slaves who found their way to Philadelphia. Somewhere along the line he acquired some learning, for by the time I came to know him he spoke and wrote fluently and gracefully. He was a good-looking man who possessed in good measure both equanimity and strong determination, a veritable rock upon whom many depended and to whom many hundreds owed their very lives.

In 1847, the same year he married, William Still became clerk of the antislavery society, managing its offices and for many years maintaining a vast correspondence with people, newspapers, and periodicals on behalf of the black man. He kept intricate records—some public, some secret—of the society's affairs and was ever ready to assist or defend any of his race who needed help. It was said that nineteen out of twenty runaways coming through Philadelphia stopped at William Still's house, and if this was not the case it was only because his house had become too dangerous as a refuge and not because he wasn't directing the escape route. Intimate, indeed, was Mr. Still's knowledge of the Underground Railroad, that great secret network of people who helped runaways from place to place along routes to safety. He recalled for me one day how the loose organization had sprung up during the 1830's and '40's to meet the needs of escaping slaves. Then, with the passage of the Fugitive Slave Act in 1850, the Underground Railroad had to become a more cautious, more tightly organized operation. The Fugitive Bill gave slavehunters a better chance to pursue escaped slaves, and it imposed stiff penalties on anyone giving aid to fugitives. A Northerner could be fined up to one thousand dollars and given up to six months in jail for helping a slave. If that Northerner fell into the hands of angry Southerners, his fate might be worse, for each state below the Mason-Dixon line had its own laws, and long jail terms were meted out. Sometimes, too, cases were handled outside the law. Murder was not unheard of. Yet hundreds of white and free colored men and women throughout the North risked helping slaves, passing them from safe hands to safe hands in groups or individually until the number of escaped fugitives numbered in the thousands.

Philadelphia had long had a Vigilance Committee, a loosely formed band of men willing to assist fugitives routed through the city or to perform any duty for the antislavery cause. By 1852, however, with the number of fugitives increasing, and greater danger involved, a smaller, more tightly knit group was needed. Late that year a nineteen-man General Vigilance Committee was formed with my Uncle Robert at its head. Within the general committee four men, led by William Still, served as acting committee. Theirs was the duty of attending to every fugitive case routed through Philadelphia. Several times a week thereafter, William Still received letters like the following from Richmond, Virginia, from Washington, D. C., from Wilmington, Delaware, or any other point to the south or west of Philadelphia:

Sunnyside, Nov. 6th, 1857

DEAR FRIEND:
Eight more of the large company reached our place last night, direct from Ercildown. The eight constitute one family of them. The husband and wife with three children under eight years of age, wish tickets for Elmira (New York). Three sons, nearly grown, will be forwarded to Phila., probably by the train which passes Phoenixville at seven o'clock of to-morrow evening the seventh. It will be safest to meet them there. We shall send them to Elijah, with the request for them to be sent there. And I presume they will be. If they should not arrive you may suppose it did not suit Elijah to send them.

We will send the money for the tickets by C. C. Burleigh, who will be in Phila. on second day morning. If you please, you will forward the tickets by to-morrow's mail as we do not have a mail again till third day. Yours hastily,

G. Lewis

William Still or one of the others on the acting committee would meet the fugitives, house them, provide them with any food, clothing, or medicine they needed, and make arrangements for the next leg of the journey north. In addition, Mr. Still habitually questioned all escaped slaves closely, making careful notes of their remarks. Where had the runaway come from? Who had been his master and mistress? What were they like? Were they religious? How did they treat their slaves? Why had the fugitive decided to run away? How had he accomplished it? What had his journey been like thus far? To all this information William Still added his own observations concerning the fugitive's color, character, and general condition. He kept these papers locked away in a safe where no one could find and use the information to track the fugitive.

"Charlotte," Mr. Still said to me one day as I lingered talking to him over the high counter in the antislavery office, "someday I'm going to write a book about these people. Someday when it's safe to tell who they are and where they've gone, I'm going to let America hear about every last fugitive. Some of them arrive here thin as rails, their bodies covered with scars from mistreatment, having come through the tortures of the damned in escaping, but their eyes are full of hope. They can see Canada and freedom. And while they're pretty ignorant on the whole—most of them have never held a pen before—they're not dumb. Nearly all are bright specimens of men and women."

"It would make a fascinating book," I agreed enthusiastically. "And it would show people that the docile, stupid slave isn't always so at all. I suppose to some degree the fugitives tell the same story over and over. Do most of them run away because of cruel treatment?"

"A lot do," William Still answered. "But you'd be surprised. That's not the only reason they give. A good many know they're about to be sold, and they're half crazy with fear of what that might mean. Some have had their wives or husbands or children taken away, and it seems to them the final straw. But a few say they've been treated well enough. They're rebelling against being a slave at all, against having to spend a lifetime doing another man's will. We get all kinds."

"Doesn't it make you wish that more could escape?" I asked urgently. "If only there were some way of helping masses of them get away instead of just this trickle who make it by the skin of their teeth."

"Maybe there will be a way eventually." William Still nodded, a faraway look in his eye. Had he knowledge of the daring scheme that John Brown was right then planning for the fastnesses of the Allegheny Mountains, his design for liberating and arming whole colonies of Negroes? William Still may well have had. But he merely changed the subject.

"What is most interesting to me, Charlotte, is not just the physical bravery of these runaways, what they go through getting here, and the beatings they risk if they're captured. They're also breaking emotional ties with the only life they've ever known. It's hard. Only last week a young slave arrived here from Richmond. Glad to be free and almost safe, yes. But he'd left his wife and three young ones on a neighboring plantation in Virginia, and he won't rest until somehow he's managed to help them north."

"Will he be able to, do you think?"

"We can try. He's going to write me when he's settled in Canada. Maybe the same people who helped him will be able to help his family. We'll have to see."

Mr. Still was usually very close-mouthed about the fugitives he helped. Although he would talk in general terms about them, he wouldn't divulge even to me, whom he knew he could trust, the details about the men, women, and children he ushered through Philadelphia. The need for secrecy was paramount, as an occasional accident all too sadly proved.

I had heard about a man named Captain William Lee of Portsmouth, Virginia, who was arrested for helping a party of slaves escape across the bay in his skiff. Captain Lee was tried, convicted under Virginia law, and sentenced to twenty-five years in the Richmond penitentiary. His wife broke under the strain and died, leaving two small children to be brought up by friends in Philadelphia. Lee himself underwent harsh treatment in prison and died there shortly before the end of the Civil War.

William Still told me an even sadder tale about a man named Seth Conklin who, in 1851, undertook to help members of William Still's own family. I have mentioned that William's mother, Charity, escaped from slavery leaving two small sons behind. Forty years later one of those sons, Peter, managed to purchase his freedom and made his way to Philadelphia. Almost the first person he met in the city was his own brother, William, whom he had never known about. While William had never known his much older brother either, he knew about him and recognized from Peter's life story who he must be. The reunion of Peter Still with his aged parents was a joyous one.

William thought his brother's experiences so interesting that he encouraged Peter to write the story of his life for the *Pennsylvania Freeman*. The story appeared under the title "The Kidnapped and the Ransomed," because Peter had always supposed himself kidnapped as a young child rather than deserted by his mother, and William advised him to perpetuate that myth to protect her. She could still have been remanded to slavery if the facts about her were known.

In his article in the *Pennsylvania Freeman* Peter Still rejoiced that he was free at last, but despaired that his wife and children were still enslaved in Alabama. A Philadelphian named Seth Conklin was strongly moved by the story. He volunteered to go to Alabama to help Peter's wife, Vina, and their three children— two sons and a daughter—escape. His plan was to play the role of a slaveholder and escort Peter's family, purportedly his slaves, eight hundred miles by steamboat to Cincinnati. If the party could move fast enough, it might outdistance the fugitives' owner. It was a daring scheme. Conklin knew that deep in the South there would be no one to help him, no one he could trust.

Before the plan was put into effect Peter Still himself returned to South Florence, Alabama, to inform his family of the rescue operation and insure their cooperation with Seth Conklin. Then Conklin, traveling as John H. Miller, set out on his perilous journey.

All went well for a time. In detailed letters to William Still, Conklin described making contact with Peter's family and laying out a course of action. He decided that his steamboat plan was too dangerous. Others had attempted the same scheme and been doomed by unpredictable delays in boat departures. Instead Conklin decided to buy a skiff in which to row his fugitives down the Tennessee River to the Ohio, up the Ohio River seventy-five miles to the Wabash, then forty-four miles up the Wabash River to New Harmony, Illinois. There he would take his party east by land to the home of David Stromon, a "conductor" on the Underground Railroad who lived at Princeton, Indiana. Stromon would route the fugitives northward through Detroit to Canada. Seth Conklin was so thorough in his preparations that he scouted the entire route in advance by steamboat and on foot. He traveled to Indiana to meet Stromon and check on his reliability, then returned to Vina and her children in Alabama.

Incredibly enough, the first part of the escape was successful. Rowing steadily for seven days and nights, with the runaways lying flat under rugs in the bottom of the skiff by day and spelling Conklin at the oars by night, the party finally reached Princeton, Indiana. They were challenged only once along the way.

From Princeton the fugitives headed north toward Detroit. But meanwhile the owner of Peter Still's family—one B. McKiernon—had raised an alert throughout the South and had sent dispatches to marshals in the principal northern cities along the main routes to Canada. Just above Vincennes, Indiana, the fugitives were apprehended. They were put in jail for a time; then McKiernon hustled them back south by steamboat, Conklin along with the Negroes. As soon as David Stromon heard of the arrest, he set out to find and aid the party, but only discovered at his every stop that Conklin and the fugitives had just preceded him.

The conclusion of the affair was a shock to all. Not far inside the Kentucky line, near the mouth of the Cumberland River, Seth Conklin suddenly disappeared. An early, hopeful rumor had it that he had jumped off the boat and escaped. But shortly afterward his drowned body was found, hands and feet in chains, skull fractured. Such was his reward for great generosity and daring. Peter's wife and children returned to slavery. An attempt was made to purchase them from McKiernon, but the price demanded was so high that nothing ever came of it.

William Still was not loath to talk about some of the bizarre fugitive cases that had passed through the hands of the Philadelphia Vigilance Committee. He described the famous case of Henry Brown of Richmond, Virginia, who elected to flee to Philadelphia in a wooden crate measuring three feet by two feet by two feet eight inches deep. A shoe dealer in Richmond, Samuel A. Smith, nailed Henry Brown into the box, secured it with hickory hoops, and sent it by overland express to a friend in the City of Brotherly Love.

In Philadelphia, J. Miller McKim, who was a white member of the Vigilance Committee, an ex-minister and key figure in antislavery activities, received notice of the shipment. He arranged to have the box delivered to the antislavery office, where he and William Still attended to uncrating the human cargo some twenty-six hours after it had left Richmond. The hoops were sawed, the lid pried, and out stepped Henry Brown, ever after known as Henry Box Brown. He shook hands all around, and before telling the details of his rough journey, paused to sing a hymn of thanksgiving, "I waited patiently for the Lord, and He heard my prayer."

The success of that escapade led others to try it. Two other Richmond slaves, William Still told me, induced Samuel Smith to box them up, but they were discovered en route to Philadelphia, and Smith was arrested and imprisoned for eight long harsh years in Virginia for his part in the affair. Then later a young woman named Lear Green stowed herself in a sea chest and escaped from Baltimore via steamer, and as recently as 1857 another young woman was sent from Baltimore to Philadelphia by railroad freight. She came closer than any of the others to perishing, being nearly suffocated by the time she was helped from her box.

Many slaves escaped in disguises. Light-colored Ellen Craft of Georgia assumed the posture of an ailing white planter attended northward by her devoted slave—in reality, her darker-colored husband, William. Fifteen-year-old Ann Maria Weems traveled north disguised as a boy. Still others had narrow escapes from their intended captors, some even fighting gun or knife battles before accomplishing their flight. The escapes described by William Still would indeed one day fill a book! Was it any wonder I found the antislavery office an interesting place to visit?

There was another service that the Vigilance Committee could and did perform for slaves. According to law, any slave freely brought into a free state by master or mistress was entitled to his freedom. William Still and others were alert to the presence in the city of any travelers accompanied by slaves. Upon hearing of such, a writ of habeas corpus was obtained, and someone from the Vigilance Committee would seek out the slave to inform him that he was free if he wished to be. Southerners were usually cautious about bringing slaves north, but occasionally they did. In 1855, Mr. Still told me, Colonel John H. Wheeler of North Carolina, the United States Minister to Nicaragua, disregarded the consequences of traveling with his servant, Jane Johnson, and her two small sons through Philadelphia en route to New York. While Colonel Wheeler stopped for dinner at a Philadelphia hotel, Jane Johnson whispered to a black employee of the hotel that she wished her freedom. Word was sent immediately to William Still, who went as quickly as he could, accompanied by a Philadelphia lawyer and Vigilance Committee member named Passmore Williamson. Williamson had a writ of habeas corpus in his hand. They discovered that Colonel Wheeler had gone aboard a steamer with his slaves and was ready to depart for New York. Still and Williamson ran aboard the boat, located the party, and in front of her angry master, informed Jane Johnson of her rights. There was a slight scuffle; then Jane and her children simply walked off the boat as free Negroes.

Hearing of the courage and daring of many blacks far less fortunate than I quickened the recovery of my health. After all, with so many interesting events going on in the world it was impossible for me to play the role of invalid too long. And as my strength returned, I felt obliged to make myself useful. While visiting Byberry late in the spring of 1858, I succumbed to the entreaties of Uncle Robert and Aunt Harriet that I come live with them to tutor their three youngest children, who were finished with grammar school now and had no good secondary school which they could attend and still live at home.

For the next year, then, I lived at Byberry. I taught, but the duties were light enough that I was able to recommence my own French and Latin studies. In addition I found time for some serious writing. No novels this time, but an article about my experiences in Salem, which the *National Anti-Slavery Standard* saw fit to publish as "Glimpses of New England," and some long, soulful poems. Two of these, "Two Voices" and "The Wind Among the Poplars," also saw publication in the *Standard*. I smile now, and blush as well, to read the yellowed clippings tucked into my old journal. Long and sentimental and relentlessly rhymed my verses were, but that was the fashion then, and my mood was quite melancholy enough to suit it.

A summer and a winter passed in the warm, genial Purvis household where there was always excitement afoot. Managing his estate and business affairs occupied Uncle Robert, while running a busy household that was rarely without guests took the attention of Aunt Harriet. I taught the younger children, studied and read and joined in the social doings of Hattie and young Robert. For exercise, and to strengthen my lungs and general constitution, I walked and rode horseback as much as possible. And of course the affairs of the Philadelphia antislavery society occupied center stage in life at Byberry, just as they did in our household on Lombard Street, so we all made frequent expeditions into the city for abolition lectures, benefits, and meetings. All in all, living with the Purvises was the best tonic a low-spirited young lady could wish for, and slowly I emerged from a long period of physical and mental depression.

As winter drained from the face of the earth, its aging ice and snow producing incredible mires in roadway and pasture, its blustery north winds subsiding before balmier southern breezes, an event occurred that spoke to our very hearts the awakening messages of spring. The first news was carried fresh from Philadelphia late on the earliest Saturday of April 1859 by the two Roberts, who had spent the day in the city.

Toward teatime we heard their carriage come up the long drive from the highway, then saw young Robert jump gracefully down and stride quickly toward the house. His greeting struck my heart with chilling familiarity.

"A fugitive's been caught. There's big excitement in the city."

"Oh, Robert, no!" The large knife with which his mother was slicing bread clattered to the floor. "What's happened? Tell us about it."

Hattie retrieved the knife while Aunt Harriet sank into the big wicker rocker, her dark eyes attentive only to her son. I propped myself upon the kitchen stool, prepared to hear of the doom of one more poor unfortunate runaway.

The story Robert told was not new. Only the details were different. Of some dozen fugitives captured in the Philadelphia area since the Fugitive Slave Bill, all had been returned to bondage. The current slave, Daniel Dangerfield, had run away from Athensville, Virginia, early in the decade and for seven years had lived in Harrisburg, Pennsylvania, under the name Daniel Webster. He had a wife and two small children, and was steadily employed. With each year that passed he must have felt a little more secure in the North, more surely out of the grasp of his former owner. Then, with no warning, he was taken prisoner while buying fish for his breakfast in the town marketplace early on that second of April morning. As three officials from Philadelphia, including the assistant United States marshal, seized Webster in the public square, a crowd began to gather. Someone ran for Daniel's wife, who came as fast as she could and began both pleading and weeping at the sight of her husband handcuffed to two white strangers. But her cries were unavailing. Daniel Webster was hustled aboard the morning train to Philadelphia.

News of the arrest preceded the fugitive's arrival in the city, so that by the time Webster was brought before Commissioner J. Cooke Longstreth the abolitionists had arranged counsel for him. Two Philadelphia lawyers of strong antislavery sentiment quickly came forward to represent Daniel Webster and to obtain a delay in the proceedings until Monday morning. All this Uncle Robert and young Robert told us while supper preparations lay abandoned on the kitchen table. Uncle Robert went off without eating to consult the Vigilance Committee, leaving the rest of us to speculate on the fugitive's chances for survival. If I could, I was determined to go into the city on Monday to witness whatever I might of the trial.

During the next day, the Sabbath, word of the arrest and pending court case spread throughout the city. The reaction among Philadelphians was surprising. For a citizenry which over the years had shown general dislike of the Negro, had forced him to build his own schools and churches, had limited him to the front platform of street cars, had deprived him of civil and natural rights, had mobbed him on this occasion, ignored him on that, the reaction was downright amazing. For some reason the case of Daniel Webster stirred the populace. Thousands rallied behind his cause with a spirit and solidarity that was heartwarming.

By Monday morning at ten o'clock—the time set for the hearing—the streets outside Commissioner Longstreth's office were crowded with people, colored and white. Hattie, young Robert, and I became separated from Uncle Robert in the crush. Things were still worse, we heard, in the commissioner's office. The room was small to begin with. This morning it was packed with the defendant, his counselors, the counsel for the claimant, several police officers, some members of the Vigilance Committee, and a group of ladies. Others were trying to press into the packed room from the hall, and everyone wanted to make himself heard.

Commissioner Longstreth banged on his desk with a book. "We cannot possibly pursue this case in these surroundings," he announced loudly. "We will adjourn to the grand jury room in the Court Building." So saying, he began herding people out the door.

When the people outside heard the word, they streamed down Chestnut and Sansom Streets, across Independence Square and into the courthouse. By the time Daniel Webster had been escorted to the scene, the jury room was jammed, and he had to be taken into an upstairs office. People surged around the prisoner, causing the police to abandon gentle ways in the process of making a way for him through the press.

Right in Daniel Webster's wake streamed the small group of ladies who had stood near him in the commissioner's office. They were middle-aged, bonneted ladies, several of whom wore Friends' garb. Their leader

was a gentle, sweet-faced woman whose visage was familiar to many in the crowd. She was Lucretia Mott,
wife of Quaker merchant William Mott, and perhaps
the most generally admired woman in Philadelphia.
Saintly-looking, benevolent, and highly intelligent, she
was deeply concerned with the rights of women and
the antislavery cause, and had organized meetings and
raised her quiet, sensitive voice in support of both
causes for many years. I knew her personally and had
heard her speak many times at antislavery meetings. I
thought her the loveliest woman alive. A beautiful
soul speaking allegiance only to conscience and to God
shone through her face, while her noble character affected and won the respect of the men and women
among whom she moved.

The police cleared the mobbed jury room, then
readmitted a sensible number of persons. Daniel
Webster and his escort of ladies, who were to remain
at his side through three days of hearings, came in
along with his attorneys, Mr. Earle and Mr. Hopper,
and the defense for the claimant, Mr. Brewster. The
day was so hot that the windows of the jury room were
thrown open. None in my party was lucky enough to
get a seat, but Uncle Robert, standing close to the
Fifth Street windows, told us later that he could see
and hear what went on quite plainly.

Mr. Brewster presented his case first. He repre-
sented Mrs. Elizabeth Simpson of Athensville, Virginia, whose slave, Daniel Dangerfield, had escaped
into Pennsylvania in November 1854. Under the Fugitive Slave Act, which Brewster read aloud, Brewster

was authorized to pursue and reclaim Mrs. Simpson's property for her. Since the slave actually belonged to Mrs. Simpson's recently deceased husband, Brewster presented to the court a copy of Mr. Simpson's will and a warrant for the arrest of Daniel Dangerfield. Several other witnesses then spoke on behalf of the alleged owner.

Next George Earle spoke for the fugitive, who because he was a Negro, was not permitted to testify in court. Earle questioned the authenticity of Mr. Simpson's will, which had several erasures and lacked a seal. Shortly, as he pointed to the lack of other documents establishing the slave's identity, his tone became emotional. Knowing his audience was with him, Earle indulged in a passionate speech on behalf of all enslaved Negroes and even accused Brewster of feeling conflict within his breast over the injustice of slavery.

The afternoon was so far advanced by the time Earle finished that Commissioner Longstreth, after advising Mr. Earle to keep personalities out of the testimony hereafter, adjourned the case until the next afternoon.

Uncle Robert managed to secure a seat next day, Tuesday, April fifth, in the sweltering courtroom. He heard the testimony of a great many Harrisburg residents, all willing to swear that Daniel Webster had come to their town as early as the winter of 1853. It was midnight before all the witnesses were done. For the following six hours, counsel summed up the case, and the watchers in the jury room, ladies included, kept their seats until dawn. Obviously exhausted by the proceedings, Commissioner Longstreth said he would reserve his decision for the afternoon. The courtroom emptied, but the abolitionists did not rest, for at noon a revivalistic prayer meeting was held on the streets of Philadelphia, as sensational an expression of public sentiment as the city had ever known.

By mid-afternoon the jury room was again packed, and the public again filled the streets outside. Commissioner Longstreth began his somber remarks from the high bench. His duty as commissioner was plain and simple, he told his tense listeners. He discountenanced all attempts of counsel to appeal to private sympathies —a dark glance at Earle here—and concentrated his judgment on three points that the claimant must prove. First, Was Daniel Dangerfield owned by Mrs. Simpson? Second, Had that slave escaped? Third, Was Daniel Webster that slave? Longstreth's voice was heavy and serious. No note of hope could be discerned. Daniel Webster, sitting amidst his phalanx of protectoresses, stared straight ahead, his face impassive but his eyes wide.

"I am satisfied with the evidence that Mr. Brewster has presented on the first two points," continued the commissioner. "I am not satisfied with the third—the identity of the slave. Not only is there clear controversy concerning the date of the escape, but the claimant has said he is searching for a fugitive three inches shorter than Daniel Webster." He paused. "I conclude, therefore, that the prisoner shall be discharged."

A sudden scream—of surprise? of joy? of suppressed emotion?—rose from the throats of the tense listeners.

The scream became a roar of approval. Applause broke out. Long and loud, standing and cheering and stamping and hugging one another in sheer delight, the people of Philadelphia congratulated one another and swooped down upon the prisoner. Daniel Webster disappeared in the crowd. No, there he was, surrounded by jubilant faces, his counsel trying to clear a path for him to the door.

Outdoors masses of rejoicing Negroes and whites picked up Daniel, placed him on the shoulders of a colossal black man who bore him up Fifth Street. Then a carriage was found. No horses needed. Two dozen men grasped the shafts and pulled the hero fugitive triumphantly through the city. Such an occasion Philadelphia had never experienced, and its citizens knew well that their united opinion had had no small influence on the outcome of the trial. How we rejoiced to hear Uncle Robert describe the tumult following the trial. And how I pored over the newspaper accounts, wishing only that all the world would read of Philadelphia's triumph.

A couple of evenings later I attended a very large antislavery meeting at Sansom Hall to celebrate Daniel's release. It was an occasion long, long, to be remembered. A crowd of Southerners was present, and ere the meeting had progressed far they created a disturbance, stamping, hallooing, and groaning, so that it was impossible to hear a word that the speakers were saying. In vain did the president strive to preserve order. The noise increased every moment, and at one point the hecklers rushed toward the platform. We thought we would be crushed, but I was not at all frightened; I was too excited to think of fear. At last the police arrived. They arrested many of the disturbers, and order was restored. Uncle Robert then made a fine speech, decidedly the most effective of the evening, and we went very late to Lombard Street to sleep.

Next day we returned to Byberry by riverboat. Uncle Robert came the overland route, bringing Daniel Webster and his family with him to get them out of the city and into seclusion. The Vigilance Committee was alarmed for Daniel's safety, having been informed that a warrant was being sworn for his rearrest, and the family must be gotten to Canada at once.

I was interested to find Daniel a sturdy, sensible man. His wife was more excitable than he, but the fact that she had buried their youngest child only ten days earlier helped explain her nervousness. Mr. Purvis arranged the Websters' secret departure, and two weeks later we heard word that they had arrived safely in Canada.

That good news was rapidly followed by a letter from my dear friend and teacher, Mary Shepard, begging me to return to Salem if my health permitted to teach under her at the Higginson Grammar School. Did I accept? You cannot imagine the alacrity with which I agreed to return to New England. To be among good friends, to have a chance to study at the normal school, to feel once more of use to society seemed very heaven to me.

Actually my life during the next three years was

quite peripatetic. I went to Salem in the spring of 1859 and took up residence with my friends, the Israel Putnams. There was no question of my troubling the Remonds, for Sarah was in Europe that year, speaking before antislavery audiences in England and France. Glowing reports of her effective oratory appeared in the antislavery newspapers. While continuing to admire Sarah's platform skills, I realized that my own talents lay in another direction. Teaching and writing were more obviously my bents.

For a full year I taught enthusiastically, and also recited at the normal school in Latin, French, German, and Algebra. Then illness again dogged my path. My eyes began to fail, and before long became so useless that I stopped teaching altogether. I rested. I tried the water cure at Worcester and discovered that hydropathic treatments restored me physically. Furthermore, the man who headed the establishment, Dr. Seth Rogers, did me worlds of good spiritually. He was a just and noble specimen of manhood and the friend of abolitionists everywhere.

By fall term 1860 I was again teaching at Higginson Grammar School, only to be shortly laid low by an attack of lung fever. A severe attack it proved to be. It brought me very close to death, then kindly permitted me to drift back this side, weak and useless but alive. At the first opportunity I crept back to Philadelphia to languish in that hateful city for a long, dreary winter.

During the same winter we began hearing alarming news from Byberry. Young Robert's health was poor. The consumption that he had long dreaded, that kept his manner delicate and his frame slim and elegant, was making its presence felt. By spring of 1861, when I was strong enough to visit the Purvises, I went to Byberry to stay. All that beautiful summer I amused my favorite cousin, and nursed him too, for his usual energy and ambition had vanished. He was inactive and weary. Together we read and talked and followed in the papers the alarming events that were convulsing the country.

National strife had reached a climax at the time of the presidential election of 1860. Sectional feelings, which were rubbed raw by fugitive slave cases, and by the fight to extend or limit slavery in the new territories, and by the taunts and charges of abolitionists and the retorts and defenses of Southerners, were further exacerbated by the different economies and ways of life that had evolved in the North and the South. The two sections looked on national life from two quite different points of view. The South was rural and agricultural, its society dominated by a small group of wealthy landowners. In the North, on the other hand, were all but one of America's large cities. Great centers of industry and manufacturing had developed. Immigrants were pouring into the North and West, increasing the population and stimulating the economy, immigrants who had little desire to live in the South and compete with slave labor. Railroads were being built, great trunk lines which opened up commerce between the East and the Mid- and Far West. The preponderance of that railroad building was occurring in the North. To protect its economy the North wanted higher tariffs and a national banking system. The South cared for neither.

Political events came to a head when the Democratic and Republican parties each met in convention during the summer of 1860 to choose their presidential candidates. The Democrats were deeply divided. A moderate group stood behind Stephen A. Douglas and his belief in popular sovereignty, the right of the people in the new territories to decide whether they should be slave or free. But Southern radicals rallied around Jefferson Davis, who believed that the power to extend slavery belonged to the federal government. The two groups would not be reconciled, so they split into two Democratic parties, each supporting a different candidate. In such a broken condition the Democrats could not hope to win against the popular figure the Republican party chose. Abraham Lincoln held moderate views on the slavery issue. In fact his conservatism infuriated some abolitionists who wanted a President who would state unequivocally that slavery was a great moral wrong and must be abolished immediately. But Lincoln was a man who wouldn't be pushed. He felt that slavery was an institution to be restricted and ultimately abolished. The more immediate, paramount issue that concerned him, however, was not slavery but preservation of the Union. "A house divided against itself cannot stand" was his famous phrase.

Notwithstanding, Southerners saw in Abraham Lincoln a man "whose opinions and purposes are hostile to slavery," and in the months following Lincoln's election, eleven Southern states chose to secede from the Union to form the Confederate States of America, with Jefferson Davis at its helm. By mid-April 1861 the country was at war.

At first, once the shock of the surrender of Fort Sumter had registered on Northern minds, a great thrill of excitement seemed to seize everyone. At last, things were in the open, sides were drawn, issues were clear. It would be a swift and glorious conflict; then all would be over, the long years of wrangling and squabbling ended. The powerful, industrial North would very shortly bring the South to heel.

In Philadelphia everything began happening at once. Regiments were formed to help meet President Lincoln's call for seventy-five thousand volunteers. Young men rushed home from college to enlist, received commissions, went here, left for there. Volunteers drilled in the city squares to the continual beating of drums. Ladies formed sewing circles to make bandages, blankets, soldiers' clothing, anything they could manufacture with enthusiastic hearts and busy needles.

Young Robert Purvis, languishing on his couch and sipping the nourishing teas and broths Aunt Harriet and I brought him, would slap the daily newsprint sharply with the back of his hand, utterly frustrated by his desire to join his contemporaries in the great fight. Not that he could have joined a regiment even if he had been well. Negroes were not allowed to become soldiers. Yet I sympathized with Robert's urge. I, too, wanted to do something to help, but felt restricted to only the quietest, most hearth-bound tasks.

Soon the news took a bleak turn. At the first great battle of Bull Run, outside Washington, D. C., the Union army met a smashing defeat and retreated in wild, hasty disorder before the more cleverly deployed Confederates. This blow was shortly followed by others east and west along the line that divided the Northern and Southern states. Casualties began to mount. Soon everyone recognized names among the dead, the wounded, the captured. War began to mean deprivation and destruction, but most of all death. Hundreds were being killed. Thousands were being killed. It became grim and unbelievable, then believable and utterly terrible.

And what about the poor slave, one of the causes of the whole miserable conflict? He seemed completely lost sight of, a negligible part of the scene of war. That man in the White House had not lifted a finger to help the black, cried Wendell Phillips, who was not the great Lincoln admirer that Garrison was. Lincoln did not seize his chance to free the slave. In fact, he even insisted on returning to the Southern border states the many slaves who made their way into Northern army camps. This was to reduce antagonism, Lincoln said. "If I could save the Union without freeing all the slaves, I would do it—and if I could save it by freeing all the slaves I would do it—and if I could do it by freeing some and leaving others alone, I would also do that," the President explained himself. Phillips and other abolitionists were exasperated.

Lincoln's hesitancy concerning the slave was shared by a great many others in the North. What was the black man really like, they wondered? Was he fit only for a life of bondage? If he were freed, would he founder? Were docility and ignorance and abjectness bred into his race, or might he indeed be capable of learning, of carrying on his own life industriously if given the opportunity? Did the Negro possess intelligence and courage in any measure comparable to the white man? Could he possibly be made ready for citizenship? These were unanswered questions. Evidently the past achievements of northern free Negroes in educating themselves and building admirable social institutions couldn't be taken into account. These free Negroes were the cream-of-the-crop blacks. In the minds and hearts of many men great fear and doubt existed concerning the mass of blacks, the 3,500,000 slaves. Even Abraham Lincoln questioned their ability to fight.

What was needed was an experiment, an opportunity to work with a group of newly freed slaves to find out what could be accomplished without the fetters of slavery and to discover how slaves might be dealt with if they were emancipated. Such a chance for experimentation came shortly after the war started.

On November 7, 1861, a Northern fleet of gunboats and troop transports captured a group of islands along the coast of South Carolina. The chief island—Port

Royal—and a half-dozen smaller ones were part of a low, sandy land mass divided by tidal rivers and creeks, known as the Sea Islands. They provided a fine, natural harbor midway up the coast between Charleston, South Carolina, and Savannah, Georgia.

On the four principal islands were cotton plantations that supported a population of about two hundred white men and ten thousand slaves. The day the Union fleet raked with fire the two dirt forts guarding the entrance to Port Royal Sound and sailed up the Beaufort River to take the town of Beaufort on Port Royal Island, the Southern landowners fled hastily, leaving all but a few of their slaves in the hands of twelve thousand Union soldiers, who quickly took over the area and established a military headquarters at Hilton Head, the entrance to Port Royal Sound.

What was the North to do with its new possessions, ten thousand "contrabands" and a huge cotton crop awaiting harvest? The War Department hastily turned over the problem to the Treasury Department, and Secretary of the Treasury Salmon P. Chase quickly appointed a young New England lawyer named Edward L. Pierce to investigate the situation at Port Royal. Secretary Chase viewed the capture of Port Royal as the opportunity the North had been groping for to test the capabilities of the slaves. Pierce, in his first report after visiting the area, supported Chase's idea that Port Royal should be the site of a social experiment for the freed Negroes. Pierce proposed a plan under which Northern superintendents would go to Port Royal to manage the cotton plantations, while Northern teachers and missionaries would be secured to teach and guide the freedmen.

The federal treasury did not have funds to support the experiment immediately, but in response to Pierce's pleas to abolitionists three charitable societies quickly formed, which launched the Port Royal experiment. In Boston, New York, and Philadelphia, Port Royal commissions undertook to find the supervisors, teachers, and ministers needed and to pay them small salaries. Many of the people who responded were young, just out of college, seminary, or medical school. Others were more experienced in teaching or preaching. None knew anything about cotton growing, but all were enthusiastic about helping the newly freed slaves. On March 3, 1862, Edward Pierce left New York aboard *The Oriental*. With him were forty-one men and twelve women, the first delegation of superintendents and teachers for Port Royal.

From the moment I heard about Port Royal, I wanted to go there. Indeed, it seemed the answer to all my desires, the chance to employ my teaching abilities to help my race. The urge to be where there was challenge and conflict, danger and duty together, was powerful in wartime. Yet in March, when that first group of pioneers sailed to the Sea Islands, I was not ready to join them. Since the preceding autumn I had been teaching at Aunt Margaretta's little school in Philadelphia. My cousin Robert Purvis' health had improved enough toward summer's end that I could leave him, and I was thankful to have something else to turn to.

Inwardly I was toying with the thought of leaving

the country altogether. Shortly after the war began, Father tied up his business affairs in Philadelphia and went to England to live. He argued that he could do nothing to help the North by remaining in this country, for he wasn't allowed to fight. But he could help by trying to persuade Englishmen to support the Northern cause, and early in the war, when it seemed that England's strong dependence on the cotton trade might bring that country to the aid of the Southern states, every ounce of persuasion to the contrary counted. I did not accompany Father when he left, because I was not yet well and Cousin Robert needed my feeble services. But as my health improved through the winter and letters from Father urged me to join him, I was increasingly tempted to seize the long-desired opportunity to go abroad.

Then in the middle of March poor Robert died. The agony of the loving hearts at Byberry was terrible to see. Attending the simple funeral at which Lucretia Mott and J. Miller McKim spoke the eulogies that Uncle Robert was too grief-stricken to utter, I wished that I had been taken instead of Robert. He had everything to live for, and I so very little. He would have made a difference to the world whereas I made none.

Still low in my mind in June, I responded to the invitation of Mary Shepard to teach the summer session at the Higginson Grammar School. Perhaps a glimpse of the sea, a walk over New England's hills, would restore my spirits. While there, in August, Mary and I paid a memorable visit to dear Mr. Whittier in Amesbury. It proved a day to be marked with a white stone, for Whittier, entertaining and charming as always, suddenly made clear to me what direction my life should take. He snorted at my melancholy, said I was feeling sorry for myself, and advised me to stop dallying in New England and hie myself to Port Royal where I might be of use to mankind. He was in touch with several of the young men and women who were working among the freedmen of the Sea Islands, and he spoke warmly and enthusiastically about their work. Whittier promised to write on my behalf to friends on the Boston Port Royal Commission. I came away rejuvenated and inspired.

Long weeks of frustration lay ahead, for no satisfaction was to be found in seeking an appointment through the Boston Commission. At last, in September, I returned to Philadelphia to consult with Mr. McKim about going under the auspices of the Philadelphia committee. Mr. McKim assured me that the only difficulty was my safe passage. My services were desperately needed. A few weeks dragged by and then, on the twenty-first of October in 1862, I received a note from Mr. McKim asking if I could be prepared to sail for Port Royal the next day. A Quaker gentleman and his daughter were going with supplies to open the first freedmen's store on the islands, and I could accompany them.

The flurry of my departure, I leave to your imagination. No tornado advanced on New York City as quickly as I, after bidding the hastiest of good-byes to friends and relatives, and throwing an assortment of clothing and personal possessions helter-skelter into a trunk. Two days later I was at sea on the steamer *United States* headed for South Carolina in the guardianship of Mr. John Hunn and his daughter, Elizabeth.

Chapter 5

~·

Columbus setting sail for the fabled Indies could scarcely have felt more full of adventure than I, standing at the bow of the *United States,* wind plucking my hair and skirts, watching New York Harbor open onto the wide, empty Atlantic. Every new venture in life should start with a voyage, thought I as the shoreline slowly evaporated from view. The sense of moving through time and space toward the unknown thrilled me for some hours. Then it was replaced by a sensation more mundane and urgent in the pit of my stomach.

Seasickness! My companion, Lizzie Hunn, and I spent one miserable sleepless night below decks in the close, rolling ladies' cabin and vowed we would hereafter avoid that dungeon at all costs. The whole second day of the voyage she and I huddled dolefully upon coils of rope on the deck, enveloped in shawls and listening in silence to the cheerful conversation of a dozen more fortunate and seaworthy passengers.

Firmly resolved not to go below again, the second night we had armchairs placed for us in a nook amidships. It was very pleasant in the open. Two young soldiers, who were returning from leave to their posts at Hilton Head, entertained us for several hours with fine singing, then left us to the society of the ocean. How wild and strange it seemed on the deck in the dark, only the dim outlines of sea and sky to be seen, only the roaring of the waves to be heard. I enjoyed it enormously. The thought that we were far, far from land added to my pleasure.

Rain was falling on our upturned faces when we woke early Sunday morning. It forced us below for a dismal day of watching gray streams of water lash the porthole glass. The weather worsened. By nightfall we were in the midst of a terrible storm. How the ship pitched and groaned, rocked and plunged, as sea upon sea broke over the bow with thunderous roars! A poor frightened waiter began pleading, "Oh, Jesus, dear Jesus" not far from where Lizzie and I had again placed mattresses in our amidships sanctuary. Later I learned that water came into the ladies' cabins, and one poor woman's baby rolled away from her in the dark. The mother was almost frantic before she found her child. All in all, I think Lizzie and I were very sensible to face the gale in the open.

By Monday morning the storm had abated, though

the sea was very rough and the wind strong. Gone at last was all trace of seasickness, and I felt refreshed and happy. I joined eagerly into conversation with the other passengers, and even accompanied them to the luncheon table, where my presence caused no difficulty, though I had half feared it might.

Next dawn we seemed to see a distant grove of trees, but it was ship masts, part of the fleet blockading Charleston Harbor. By noontime that day, a warm, murky October twenty-eighth, we were steaming past the outermost Sea Islands of South Carolina, our destination.

What had I expected when we arrived at Hilton Head, Port Royal? Surely I had been well informed concerning the warm climate and the sandy terrain, the presence of an army camp and the black contraband inhabitants of the region. Yet the sandy point of Hilton Head appeared more desolate than I had imagined, its low, bare outline broken only by small white-roofed houses newly built for the freed people. The motley assemblage of officers, soldiers, and Negroes on the wharf struck me as an exceedingly forlorn welcoming committee.

After signing an oath of allegiance to the government and being warned of the dire penalties of treason, the Hunns and I left the *United States* at Hilton Head and boarded a smaller steamer, which carried us up Port Royal Harbor to the town of Beaufort. The boat was the *Flora,* the steamer of Brigadier General Rufus Saxton, military commander of the Port Royal experiment. By great good fortune General Saxton was

aboard, and we were introduced to that affable gentleman. "Gen'l Saxby," as the black people affectionately
called him, had in July taken the reins of the experiment from Edward Pierce and assumed responsibility
for rectifying some of the early problems that beset the
project. From the general we heard about the eventful
eight months that preceded our arrival. As his conversation enlightened John Hunn, Lizzie, and me, the
Flora steamed up the Beaufort River, and our eyes absorbed the strange landscape of our new home.

The freedmen of Port Royal, General Saxton told
us, were as backward a group of Negroes as could be
found in the South. They had been brought directly to
the Sea Islands from Africa and had lived for several
generations physically isolated from the South Carolina mainland. They saw few white people, only the
plantation owners on the islands, and the great majority had spent their lives as ignorant field hands. Docile
and superstitious, they tended to be, and they spoke a
broken, almost unintelligible English jargon. I quickly
discovered it took time and attention to decipher the
people's strange, garbled speech.

As slave standards went, General Saxton said, the
blacks at Port Royal had not been badly treated by the
"Secesh"—the name given the white owners. The
slaves were provided with a diet of potatoes and corn,
supplemented occasionally by molasses and meat. Fish,
oysters, and crabs could be had for the taking in the
tidal inlets, and most slaves kept pigs and chickens
whose produce they sold for such luxuries as coffee,

sugar, and tobacco. On most plantations the slaves received cloth for two sets of garments each year—cotton for summer and wool for winter—besides shoes and handkerchiefs and cotton for undergarments. Every three years or so they received a new blanket. The slave quarters, usually located a quarter mile back of the main house on each plantation, were small cabins —some with floors and chimneys, some without.

Recognizing the value of their slaves, the Southern owners had looked after the health of the sick and had provided half tasks and time off for pregnant women and nursing mothers. Three free days at Christmas comprised the one big annual holiday, although a free day and extra rations might be given at those seasons of heaviest labor, the spring hoeing and autumn harvest of the cotton, when slaves worked from "day clean to first dark."

"It's a somewhat inferior grade of cotton that grows here." General Saxton pointed with a sweep of his hand toward some straggling cotton fields along the riverbanks. Indeed I, who had expected to see fields bursting with great snowballs, was inclined to agree with him.

"This sandy soil and the salt water produce a long-fibered cotton," the general went on, "and the crops are quite moderate. Every once in a while there's an extraordinary year when profits are very large. But the poor years offset that, and on the whole the economy hasn't especially boomed on the islands. Enough to support the plantation owners on their land and to provide most of them with another nicer home in Beaufort, where they could take their families during the hottest months, the fever season."

"The government got a decent price for the cotton crop that was harvested after we took the islands," Mr. Hunn reminded the general.

"Thank goodness, yes," Rufus Saxton replied. "And the money has been used to pay the freedmen wages and to buy seed and tools and animals. What you see growing now had a pretty late start, but Edward Pierce had his problems getting things organized, so to me it's a wonder there's a crop growing at all."

General Saxton went on to describe how, on the day Port Royal was captured, the day of "gun shoot" as the people called it, the plantation owners had fled to the mainland in great haste. Women, children, household possessions, and house servants were hurried into boats to escape the Northern troops. Slaveowners left their slaves and livestock and crops, but hurriedly took, if they could, their teams and farm implements. The Union troops who occupied the islands soon confiscated the cows and sheep left on the plantations, along with the food stores, so the frightened, abandoned Negroes found themselves in the hands of strangers with little to eat and no sense of what to do next.

"Within a few months' time Edward Pierce surveyed the desperate situation here, formulated a good plan, and went North to find men enough to manage the two hundred plantations on the islands," General Saxton told us admiringly. "In quick order he rounded up some mighty zealous workers. It's the missionary fervor of the volunteers that's really responsible for our success here. Most of the Northern men and women who came were prepared to labor long and hard under poor conditions, and they have. The men were made superintendents of the plantations; the women set up schools. Pierce parceled out several plantations apiece to the superintendents. All were totally inexperienced at raising cotton, and in addition they found they had to talk the newly freed slaves into going back to work in the fields."

"That wasn't easy, from what Mr. McKim told us after his visit here last summer," I said.

"It certainly wasn't," laughed General Saxton. "And it still isn't. After all, the Negroes were pretty suspicious of the Northerners. The Secesh had told them horrible tales about what Northerners would do to them—sell them into slavery in Cuba and the like. Then they saw the Union soldiers loot the plantation homes and confiscate the livestock and tools and food supplies. So when new superintendents called them freedmen but wanted them to do their old slave labors in the cotton fields, they hung back. The difference was, of course, that the Northerners promised to pay wages and promised not to use the lash. Finally, by working through the Negro drivers, the gang leaders, the superintendents got the people to harvest the ripe cotton and plant a new crop. They were hampered every step of the way by lack of hoes and plows and by not having any money to pay the promised wages. But slowly things have improved. The people have been paid something now, though not all they've earned, and they're eager to buy things to improve their way of life. That's why you're highly welcome here, sir." The general bowed to Mr. Hunn.

"I hope I've brought enough to satisfy them," John Hunn said in his quiet voice. Throughout our journey he had kept track of innumerable trunks and boxes containing merchandise with which he planned to open the first store on the islands. It was to be a non-profit enterprise, with new and used goods sent from Philadelphia. John Hunn, long a friend of the oppressed, had once paid a heavy fine for helping fugitives in Pennsylvania. Now his strong Quaker convictions had brought him among the freedmen of Port Royal to do what he could to better their lives.

"You'll be the most popular man on the islands, I've no doubt," General Saxton assured him. Then he turned to Lizzie and me. "I hope you're prepared for hard work, my dears. Miss Towne and Miss Murray and others of your predecessors have been unstinting in their devotion to teaching and doctoring and helping the women and children on the islands. In fact, if the women hadn't been doing their good work among the people, I doubt if we would have won their trust at all. Particularly we would never have weathered the call-up of Negro recruits."

"I've heard something about that," Mr. Hunn interjected. "What happened exactly?"

"Well, it boils down to what you might call a well-intentioned mistake on the part of General Hunter," General Saxton said good-humoredly, referring to the man who as commander of the Department of the

South was his military superior. "General Hunter has always been an ardent abolitionist, and for years he's objected to the regulations that prevented Negroes from serving in the military. Being an ardent soldier as well, he viewed such discrimination as the height of underprivilege. So back in May, just as Pierce's superintendents had gotten their plantations operating, with laborers back in the fields and all, General Hunter issued an order that all able-bodied freedmen were to report to Hilton Head for military training. He honestly thought they'd jump at the chance to be on the same footing with white men."

"But they didn't look at it that way?" asked Lizzie shyly.

"They certainly didn't," boomed General Saxton. "The freedmen thought it was the first step toward mass deportation to Cuba, the very thing the Secesh had warned them about. They were miserable about being separated from their families. And the superintendents were angry, too, because only women and infirm men were left to work in the fields. The best laborers were rounded up and taken away. It caused quite an uproar. Pierce protested to General Hunter and to Secretary Chase in Washington, and Washington decided there was too much conflict of authority here between the military and the civilian. So management of the experiment has been reorganized under direction of the Secretary of War, and that's how I came into the picture."

"What happened to the freedmen? Are they still being recruited?" John Hunn wanted to know.

"No. Except for one small company, they returned to their homes. And they didn't get any wages for the time spent as soldiers either," General Saxton replied. "But the funny thing is, we're really shy of troops to guard these islands properly. We could use another regiment here, and it makes sense for it to be a black regiment. Well, Congress, as you know, passed legislation early this past summer authorizing the military to make use of contraband Negroes at last. It was high time. So many slaves were being captured or freed or were coming through the lines to the Union side they were causing quite a problem. Lincoln was insisting they be returned, or at least not be involved in the fighting, and it was getting difficult to keep them busy —let alone, fed and clothed and housed. But now their services can be used, and I for one am convinced they'll prove valuable. I truly believe freedmen will make fine soldiers, and they ought to be given the chance to fight for their freedom. Anyway I went to Washington to talk with Secretary of War Stanton about forming a volunteer regiment of Negro soldiers here at Port Royal, and I received his blessing. Volunteering, of course, makes a big difference to the people here, and so does giving them some wages, which the government has promised it will pay this time. So far, more than four hundred freedmen have enlisted, and I'm looking for just the right man to command the regiment. I have an excellent fellow—from my native Massachusetts—in mind."

The mention of Massachusetts set my mind tingling. How far away it seemed—the other side of the earth now. I would have loved to indulge in a conversation with the general about New England, but saw it would have to wait for another time.

We had turned into a widened portion of the river. The steamer was slowing for landing at a not too distant wharf, beyond which clustered the buildings of Beaufort. The passengers began to stir about their baggage, and Mr. Hunn excused himself to look after his boxes and barrels. General Saxton said farewell to Lizzie and me, wishing us good luck and inviting us to visit him at his headquarters south of Beaufort whenever we found the time.

"Every bit as if he had nothing to do but wait on lady callers," giggled Lizzie later, enjoying the memory of her first invitation from a brigadier general.

At Beaufort we were met by Reverend Mansfield French, an agent of the New York Freedman's Relief Commission, who informed us our journey was still not over. We must cross the river by boat to Ladies Island, which touched St. Helena, the island where I was to teach in Miss Towne's newly established school and Mr. Hunn and Lizzie would establish their store.

While waiting for the boat, Mr. French showed us about Beaufort. The houses along the main street, fronting the bay, were large, handsome wooden dwellings with spacious southern piazzas, surrounded by fine trees. The public library had become a shelter for some of the freed people, and we speculated on what the Rebels might think of this turn of events. We saw the marketplace, where slaves were sometimes sold, but learned that the buying and selling at auction usually took place in Charleston. The houses in the smaller streets looked dismantled and desolate.

We saw only a few soldiers and freedmen, though little colored children were playing in the streets, looking as happy as children ought to look with the evil shadow of slavery no longer hanging over them. The few Union officers we met did not impress us favorably. When they found we had come here to teach, they spoke flippantly and sneeringly of the blacks, and took the trouble to assure us of the danger of Rebel attacks and the alarming prevalence of yellow fever as well. We were glad to leave them to take tea at the handsome house occupied by Mr. French and several others involved in the Port Royal experiment. There we talked pleasantly and admired the rich, dark, shining foliage of a magnificent magnolia tree in the yard until the call came that our boat was leaving.

To my great joy I found we were to be rowed to Ladies Island by a crew of Negro boatmen, a delightful experience which convinced me I had arrived in a new life. Picture an extravagant crimson sunset, with color and clouds reflected in smooth, calm water. Add to it the rich, sonorous voices of the boatmen breaking full upon the evening stillness as their oars dipped with steady, languid rhythm into the tidal river:

> Jesus make de blind to see
> Jesus make de deaf to hear
> Jesus make de cripple walk
> Walk in, dear Jesus,
> No man can hender me.

Lucy McKim, daughter of J. Miller McKim and my good friend in Philadelphia, had been so impressed by the singing of the Negroes on her visit to Port Royal with her father during the recent summer that she was planning to publish a collection of slave songs. She had told me I could expect to be deeply moved by the singing, and indeed I was. The melodies were simple and the words, even those I couldn't distinguish, were repetitious and sung in a minor key. No attempt was made at harmony. Yet the sweetness and earnestness and varied intonation of the deep voices were extraordinarily beautiful. I could have listened forever.

It was dark when we landed on Ladies Island, and darker than dark as we drove along lonely roads in the carriage Miss Towne had sent to the landing for Mr. Hunn, Lizzie, and me; but we were jubilant, and all sang "John Brown's Body" lustily. The driver of the carriage was a freedman named Harry, who was very talkative. He expressed surprise that we had never heard of him before, and seemed to think everyone in the North knew about him. We later learned that a Northern visitor who had toured the island had publicly mentioned Harry, and Harry imagined himself quite famous. Despite this touch of vanity Harry was, we soon discovered, one of the best and smartest men on the island. Beside him on the driver's seat perched a little boy named Cupid, whose duty was the opening and shutting of the gates that barred our path every quarter mile or so. Cupid was as quiet as Harry was vocal, but he followed our conversation avidly, and I could see his frequent grin even in the dark.

At last we arrived at the Thomas Fripp plantation, where Superintendent Richard Soule, Miss Laura Towne, Miss Ellen Murray, and others quartered in that household received us before a cheerful grate fire. Everything seemed homelike, yet I was possessed by a strong sense of unreality, compounded by weariness from traveling. It was a great relief to be shown where I might lay my head for the night, and I sank readily to sleep, deep in the heart of rebeldom.

I believe I have rarely been happier in my life than those first weeks on St. Helena. Everything was new and fresh to my eyes, so that I went about in a perpetual state of awe. If there had been six of me I couldn't have accomplished all there was to do, and nothing buoys a person's spirits like feeling useful. Almost anything I did earned gratitude from the people or my fellow workers. My days were so full that at night I fell into an exhausted sleep, oblivious to makeshift accommodations, and in the morning found myself on my feet again scarcely aware that a night's respite had intervened.

The Hunns and I stayed at the Fripp plantation but a few days before moving to our own quarters, a more dilapidated plantation called Oaklands, three miles nearer the center of St. Helena Island and within walking distance of the brick Baptist church where I was to teach school. At Oaklands Lizzie Hunn and her father established their store.

Our first view of the main house was disheartening. Up a weed-choked drive we went, into a neglected yard, and there saw a paintless one-story building with low-roofed piazza running its full length. The garden was badly overgrown, yet roses bloomed, and so did the feathery, fragrant acacia, while ivy crept along the ground and under the house. Oaklands had been the home of a rebel physician named Dr. Sams. In a small dark entry we found shelves of old medicine bottles, some still filled with his nostrums.

Though the exterior of Oaklands remained guiltless of whitewash or paint as long as I lived there, the freed people on the place soon scrubbed and whitewashed the interior for us, and after Mr. Hunn had chosen the largest room for his store, Lizzie and I worked at making the rest of the house presentable as living quarters.

Our furniture consisted of a bedstead, two bureaus, three small pine tables, and two chairs—one broken. We set to work arranging them. Cupid the elder, father of the little gate opener, was to be our indispensable right-hand man. He shortly brought in a load of wood to make a fire in our open grate. A good fireplace and chimney were necessary in South Carolina, for winters there proved colder than we anticipated, and even woolen clothing could not protect us completely from the chilling winds that filtered through cracks in the floor and crevices around windows and doors.

Cupid the elder was a small wiry figure, stockingless, shoeless, out at the knees and elbows, who wore indoors and out the remnant of an old straw hat. His face was nearly black, very ugly, but with a shrewd expression and a particular brightness to his eyes. He proved capable of taking excellent care of us, for he became our oysterman, coachman, postal clerk, and indispensable jack-of-all-trades. When our chimney at first refused to draw, he poked assiduously at its sooty interior, all the while heaping upon it highly original and uncomplimentary epithets. Lizzie and I stood giggling at his performance, half suffocated by smoke, until at last the blaze took hold and burned properly. When shortly afterward our cook, a large, cheerful, neat-looking black woman named Arametta, appeared with eggs and hominy for luncheon, we felt we had become an established household.

During the ensuing days Lizzie and I took pictures and books out of our trunks. We made a table cover from red and yellow handkerchiefs found among the store goods, and we constructed a carpet from a length of red and black woolen plaid. A calico cushion stuffed with cornhusks occupied the lounge built for us by Ben, the carpenter. Our greatest luxury was a cornhusk mattress, which could be properly appreciated only after having slept several nights on the bare slats of a bedstead as Lizzie and I tried to do. Cornhusks were our bed of roses.

My foremost desire on arriving was to come to know the people of St. Helena, the newly freed slaves who had spent their lives in unceasing, dreary labor in the cotton fields under the lordship of the lash. Until now the only slaves I had known had been fugitives who had sought freedom. Freedom had come to the slaves of the Sea Islands. What changes, I wondered, had it wrought on their lives and spirits?

Oaklands was a small plantation, with no more than

eight or nine black families living on it. Their quarters, to which Lizzie and I began making daily visits, were a few rods back of the main house. On this, as on most of the other plantations, the Negro houses were miserable little huts with nothing comfortable or homelike about them. They usually had two very small rooms with dirt floors, and were lighted only by their open door and paneless windows. In such a place a mother, father, and large family of children were obliged to live, and one can imagine the difficulties maintaining neatness and order in such crowded conditions. We hoped better houses would be built for them before long.

What appeared at first to be a sea of smiling faces soon distinguished itself into familiar countenances as we came to know the people individually and sorted out the family and social relationships. If they were surprised to see a Northern Negro in their midst, they didn't say so. I was obviously set apart from them by my lighter coloring, for the Port Royal freedmen were very dark-skinned with rarely a mulatto among them.

Harry, who had driven us across the island that first night, was foreman of our plantation. He was a man of great natural intelligence, who soon began coming to me every night for a reading lesson. He learned rapidly. In fact, I never saw anyone more determined to learn than he. After the lesson he would stay to answer questions about the islands and the lives the slaves had led. He loved to talk about "gun shoot" and how "Massa run when he hear de fust gun."

"Why didn't you go with him, Harry?" I asked.

"Oh, Miss, Massa try to 'suade me. He tell we dat de Yankees would shoot we, or would sell we to Cuba, an' do all de wust tings to we, when dey come. 'Bery well, Sar,' says I. 'If I go wid you, I be good as dead. If I stay here, I can't do no wust; so if I got to dead, I might's well dead here. So I'll wait for de "dam Yankees." ' Lor', Miss, I knowed he wasn't tellin' de truth all de time."

"How did you know?"

"Dunno, Miss. Somehow we hear de Yankees our friends, an' dat we be free when dey come, an' 'pears like we believe *dat*."

Cupid had told us that Dr. Sams had dared to come back after "gun shoot," at the risk of capture, and that he had ordered the Oaklands people to get the furniture of the big house together and take it to a plantation on the other side of the creek and wait for him there.

"So," said Cupid, "dey could jus' sweep us all up in a heap an' put us in de boat. An' he telled me to take Patience—dat's my wife—an' de chil'en down to a certain pint, an' den I could come back if I chose. Jus' as if I was gwine be sich a goat!"

Cupid's look and gesture of contempt were devastating. He and the rest of the people, instead of obeying their master, left the place and hid in the woods. When Dr. Sams came to look for them not one was to be found. Cupid's pleasure at being free knew no bounds. He spoke of his experiences over and over again.

Celia was one of my favorite people on the place.

She was a cripple, once the victim of such bitter cold that both her legs had had to be amputated below the knees. Yet she got about actively. She had a pretty, gentle face and was extremely kind. In every household when there was illness or trouble, Celia's sympathy was first to arrive, and her services were the most acceptable. Her daughter Rose, who was our maid of all work, had inherited her sweet disposition.

I have mentioned Arametta, our cook, washer, and ironer, whose cheerful competence sustained us all. She had an adorable little niece, her namesake, who followed auntie about our house and charmed everyone with her lovely voice, her delicate features, and her demure, kittenish ways. I yearned to adopt her.

The letter of instruction given me and other women sent to the islands by the Philadelphia Port Royal Relief Association stated, "All teachers, in addition to their regular work, are encouraged to interest themselves in the moral, religious and social improvement of the families of their pupils; to visit them in their homes; to instruct the women and girls in sewing and domestic economy; to encourage and take part in religious meetings and Sunday schools." It was a tall order, and one that could have occupied me full-time.

An epidemic of whooping cough was going on among the children when we first arrived, and Lizzie and I checked constantly on the health of the little sufferers, carrying them Miss Laura Towne's medicines and other small comforts. "Glad you come we house" would greet us as we entered a cabin, often dark and smoky if its shutters were closed against the weather.

"Too glad, too glad," Tillah or Ruby or Venus or another mother would add in characteristic island fashion.

I enjoyed talking with the women—hearing the daily gossip of the people, coming to know their way of life—and I especially loved the many children who ran about freely and nearly naked. Soon I had several favorites and found time to cut out little dresses for them to eke out their sparse wardrobes. The people were grateful for any attention, from soap to ABC lesson, and they insisted on repaying the least kindness. Lizzie and I invariably went home bearing eggs or potatoes or tania, the large queer-looking potatolike root which I never learned to like. Nevertheless we welcomed such gifts, for our diet was quite limited and variety in any form was pleasant.

In the evenings the children often came in to sing and shout for us. These "shouts" were the chief entertainment among the people. They were almost indescribable, and had to be seen and heard to be truly appreciated. The children formed a ring and moved in a kind of shuffling dance, singing all the time. A few stood apart, singing energetically, with hands clapping and feet stamping, rocking their bodies to and fro. These were the musicians, with whose performance the shouters kept perfect time. Prince, a large black boy from a neighboring plantation, often led our shouts, and his performance was practically a gymnastic exhibition. He couldn't keep still for a moment. The songs were the people's own hymns, which were

always sad in nature. There would be our cherubic little Arametta with her sweet voice, dancing and singing,

> What make ole Satan follow me so?
> Satan got nuttin' 't all fur to do wid me.
>> Hold your light,
>> Hold your light,
> Hold your light on Canaan's shore.

> (*chorus*)

> Tiddy [sister] Rosa, hold your light!
> Brudder Tony, hold your light!
> All de member, hold bright light
>> On Canaan's shore!

The children were but imitating the grown-ups,
who held shouts on most of the larger plantations,
though they didn't on ours. The shouts took place several times a week in the "praise house," that building
on a plantation used by the slaves for their own services of worship. Visiting once at Seaside, another plantation on St. Helena, we attended a praise meeting.
First there was singing and praying and preaching by
an old black preacher. Then after solemn handshaking
among the congregation, everyone readied for a grand
shout. The singing was led by Maurice, a blind man
with a remarkable voice whose excitement and ges-
tures could scarcely be controlled. The red glare of a
burning pineknot threw the dancers' frantic shadows

on the blackened walls of the large gloomy room. It was a wild, strange, deeply impressive sight, and the singing carried it effectively into my memory.

> Jesus call you. Go in de wilderness,
>   Go in de wilderness, go in de wilderness,
> Jesus call you. Go in de wilderness
>   To wait upon de Lord
>   (*chorus*)
>
> Go wait upon de Lord,
> Go wait upon de Lord,
> Go wait upon de Lord, my God,
> He take away de sins of the world.
>
> Jesus awaitin'. Go in de wilderness,
>   Go in de wilderness, go in de wilderness,
> All dem chil'en go in de wilderness,
>   To wait upon de Lord.

The shouters would sing the songs through several times until they felt ready for a new one, and their supply seemed endless. Some favorites we heard again and again. "Down in the Lonesome Valley" was sung at almost every gathering, as was one of the few happy songs they had, one they had begun singing in the twelve months since "gun shoot":

> No more peck o' corn for me,
>   No more, no more,—
> No more peck o' corn for me,
>   Many tousand go.

> No more driver's lash for me,
> No more, no more—
> No more driver's lash for me,
> Many tousand go.

That night at Seaside as Lizzie and I traced our homeward path from the praise house to the main house, the lantern flickering and our lungs tingling from the cool night air, we were followed by the phrases of the song growing fainter and fainter behind us. "No more pint o' salt for me," "No more hundred lash for me," were still echoing in our heads as we prepared for bed.

Maurice's blindness, Harry told us later, had been caused by a blow on the head from a loaded whip wielded by Maurice's master in a fit of anger. The master hadn't been a hard man, Harry assured us. He was only cruel when he worked himself into a passion.

By now Harry was making good progress at his lessons. He was already in the third reader, and both he and I were proud of his growing skill. When an evening's session was over Harry would sit and talk with John Hunn, Lizzie, and me, telling us about life on the islands during slavery and answering our questions. Several times I tried to get him to explain about the spirituals sung by the people. Where did they come from? Who learned them or made them up and taught them to the others? It seemed obvious that the songs came out of the experiences of the slaves and that they were bound into the people's religion. But just how did a spiritual get started? I wondered. Harry didn't seem to know. Several times he shrugged off my question, but he must have done some thinking about it.

"I tell you, it dis way," he said at last one night. "Dey make 'em, miss. My master, he call me up and order me short peck o' corn and hundred lash. My friends, dey see it and be sorry. When dey come de praise meetin' dat night, dey sing 'bout it. Some's bery good singers. Dey knows how, and dey wuk it in, wuk it in, till it right, and dat's de way."

It was a good explanation, the best I ever got, though I questioned other of the people from time to time. Another enlightening conversation with Harry ensued when I asked him one evening about "the promised land" so often mentioned in the songs. Weren't the island people glad to be free, I asked him, so they need no longer look only to death and to heaven for the end of their troubles? Harry quickly corrected me. To my amazement I learned that the promised land didn't always mean heaven but referred to Africa. My eyes opened wide as Harry told me about several boatloads of slaves sent from the Sea Islands to Liberia by the American Colonization Society several years before. In Liberia the slaves were free. All slaves, said Harry, dreamed of going "home" to Africa. The desire found its way into many of their spirituals.

"Harry," I said, reacting to this revelation with confusion and surprise, "you've been a slave, but you're an American, too! You were born and raised in this country. It's part of you. I was born and raised here. So was my father and my grandfather. The colonization society begged my grandfather to go to Liberia, but he refused. He knew he belonged in America, just as you do. He fought hard against deporting American Negroes to an African colony. Wouldn't you far rather be free here than leave the country of your birth?"

Harry didn't answer me at once. He played with the edge of his hat a moment and shifted his weight a couple of times while he considered my outburst. Finally he said softly, "Miss, you not a slave. You neber been a slave. You been free."

With that he went, leaving me to ponder what he had said, my thoughts illuminated by a single flickering candle, which had been stuck for want of a candlestick into a potato. At last I was aware of the wide gulf between me and the Southern slaves for whom I had always felt such sympathy and brotherly love, with whom I had, indeed, always identified myself. The truth came slowly. I and my kind, the Northern free Negro, existed somewhere between black and white, in a limbo of our own. We were black: we had tasted some of the abuse heaped upon the slave, but we were free. We could afford to scorn colonization as a lesser degree of freedom. While white men looked down upon the free Negro's dark skin, slaves and freedmen recognized his comparative privilege. For the first time I saw myself in a new light, through Harry's eyes, and realized I was neither slave nor white, nor ever could be. What direction was I traveling then, and what direction would all black men go once they were free? No answer. I had always assumed the white man's way was my goal, the goal of all Negroes. But was it really attainable? And was it the right goal for us? Perhaps Harry's vision was keener than my own. Feeling very small and lonely, and subdued by doubts I had never had before, I picked up my makeshift candlestick and by its wavering light took myself to bed.

My chief occupation at St. Helena Island was, of course, teaching at the Baptist church, where Miss Towne and Miss Murray had established the island school. The brick building stood in the center of a lovely grove of live oaks. I was unprepared for the beauty of these trees, having heard nothing about them in the North. The oaks were large, with glossy green leaves, but what was remarkable about them was that from every branch hung heavily draped moss in pendants four or five feet long. The effect was both decorative and funereal and made the trees extraordinarily beautiful.

The road along which I walked to school each mid-morning was the loveliest byway imaginable. It was lined almost its entire length by trees—on one side by tall, stately pines, on the other by live oaks hung with moss. Climbing the tree trunks and forming canopies from hedge to treetop were vines of many kinds, some, like the jessamine, bearing fragrant flowers. The hedges glowed with scarlet cassena berries, and mistletoe could be glimpsed here and there. Birds, chief among them the mockingbird, sang and flitted about this enchanted woodland. The air was soft and scented with the delicious odor of brown pine needles, which covered the roadway underfoot. But once one was out of the woods the flat terrain was sandy and the roads bad. I had hard work plodding through sand the last stretch of my journey to the grove that held the church school.

My assignment, unless Miss Murray or Miss Towne was absent, was the care and teaching of the littlest children, the babies as we called them. It was no easy task. Some were too young to learn the alphabet, having been brought to school because the older children, in whose care their parents left them while at work in the fields, could not come without them. It took me several days to learn to cope with their perpetual motion. I wrote Aunt Margaretta asking her to send me alphabet blocks and colorful ABC cards, but knew it would be weeks or months before such treasures could arrive. Mail deliveries were highly irregular, depending upon passing steamers, and we soon learned not to count on hearing regularly from friends and loved ones in the North.

In all my experience I had never seen children so eager to learn. Coming to school seemed a delight and recreation to them. The older ones worked in the fields from early morning until near noon, then came to school until midafternoon as bright and anxious to learn as if they hadn't been toiling in the hot sun at all. Some were learning their numbers and their ABC's. Others, who had been taught during the summer, were progressing in *Wilson's Reader* and *Towle's Speller,* and some were already reciting their six-times table in multiplication.

Of course, there were stupid ones, but the majority learned rapidly enough to make me indignant at the thought of people who considered the black race inferior. Visitors to our school were always amazed to see the obvious progress the children were making, to see how eagerly pencils squeaked on highly prized slates. But because our pupils were unused to intellectual concentration, we had to work hard to keep their interest, which made teaching more fatiguing than I had ever known it. We were short of teachers, short of supplies, and handicapped by teaching 140 pupils in one room, but the reward was great, and many a good report of us was carried back North.

Toward the end of our school day the children practiced memorizing and reciting the Psalms; then we closed with singing. How the children loved that! Like their elders, they couldn't refrain from putting their full body into their singing. Small heads would begin to nod, feet to slap, hands to clap, and bodies to sway, all in rhythm to their rich, sweet tones. Their favorite, which quickly became mine, was "Down in the Lonesome Valley." It had a beautiful, touching melody.

> My sister, you want to git religion,
>   Go down in de Lonesome Valley;
> My brudder, you want to git religion,
>   Go down in de Lonesome Valley.

> *(chorus)*

> Go down in de Lonesome Valley,
> Go down in de Lonesome Valley, my Lord,

Go down in de Lonesome Valley,
    To meet my Jesus dere!

Oh feed on milk and honey
Oh feed on milk and honey, my Lord,
Oh feed on milk and honey,
    Meet my Jesus dere!

Oh John he brought a letter,
Oh John he brought a letter, my Lord.
Oh Mary an' Marta read 'em,
    Meet my Jesus dere!

(*chorus*)

Go down in de Lonesome Valley, etc.

The children's natural talent for music made me yearn to teach them "John Brown's Body" and Whittier's "Song of the Negro Boatmen." They had already learned "My Country 'Tis of Thee," and Miss Murray was instructing them in "Sound the Loud Timbrel," though they seemed less enthusiasic about these imported melodies than their own familiar songs.

We held no school Saturdays and Sundays, and I usually spent the former helping Mr. Hunn in the store. The first few weeks he was so besieged by customers he didn't really have time to arrange his stock. As quickly as he unpacked a box, its contents would be sold to the freedmen who crowded around at all hours of the day, bringing gold and silver coins they had been earning and hoarding since "gun shoot."

Working in the store was fun and exhausting. Since

Saturday afternoon was a holiday on the islands, half the people of St. Helena headed for Mr. Hunn's, and all seemed to want to be waited on at once. Pots and kettles, household utensils, brightly colored fabrics and head handkerchiefs, crossed the counter at a great rate, and there was a constant run on those luxuries with which the people "pleasured" themselves—sugar, tobacco, and molasses.

Cupid was Mr. Hunn's most valuable assistant, for he presided over the molasses barrel in the yard, haranguing and scolding the eager, noisy crowd that collected around him. Up the road leading to Oaklands came a procession of men, women, and children carrying on their heads cans, jugs, pitchers, and bottles in which to carry home molasses. I marveled at the ease with which the people could carry on their heads everything from heavy bundles of wood or pails of water to rakes and hoes.

At rare moments the crowd would thin, and there would be a chance to visit with some of the customers. Then it was that I heard stories of how the people had fared before and since "gun shoot." Some of those who had been forced by the Secesh to go to the mainland had returned, and they enjoyed telling of their difficult escapes, of traveling by night and making or stealing rafts and boats to cross the myriad waterways of the area. One fugitive described his experiences to me in the store one day in blood-chilling detail. His wife, standing proudly beside him, concluded his tale by saying it had been almost "like death" for her and the children to suddenly lay eyes on him again.

I think the true dignity and sensitivity of the people was best expressed by a very old man named Scipio, who came into the store dressed in a complete suit of Brussels carpeting, originally the floor covering of his master's house. Scipio—who was also called Dr. Crofts for a reason I never learned—was rejoicing to Mr. Hunn about the new state of things on the island. "Don't hab me feelins hurt now," he exclaimed. "Used to hab me feelins hurt all de time. But don't hab 'em hurt now no more." For him freedom meant the joy of being respected as a human being, as a man, and I was grateful that this pleasure could grace his declining years.

One late autumn day I went with Laura Towne on a doctoring visit to The Corner, a small Negro community not far from the school. Old Suzy was matriarch of the settlement, and a most interesting character she was. She accompanied us from cabin to cabin as Miss Towne distributed medicines and advice in the homes of several sick children. Old Suzy was steeped in medicinal folklore and over the years had healed many sick people with her homemade brews and potions. Miss Towne was respectful of Suzy's knowledge of herbs and cures, for some of her remedies were highly beneficial. Suzy was every bit as interested in the strange pills and powders dispensed from the vials in Laura Towne's black doctor's case. She asked endless questions about them. The conversations between Old Suzy and Miss Towne had come to include a great deal of banter concerning old ways and modern ways of doctoring. I enjoyed the friendly sparring between the old Negress, who had raised many children and many more grandchildren, and the thirty-year-old white woman who was using her medical training to such humane advantage among the freedmen.

That same day I saw for the first time a newborn child, and could scarcely tear myself away from the sight of such tiny features and fingers. How could such a frail being possibly survive? I marveled. Infant mortality was high on the Sea Islands, where fevers, epidemics, and lockjaw took a high toll of the young. I prayed that this child might live. Perhaps I would even have her in my classroom someday. I thought of a certain scrap of bright pink cloth that had come in a box from Philadelphia and would make a lovely tiny first dress for the baby if I could find an hour to stitch it.

"We must go, Charlotte," Miss Towne said finally, snapping together the clasps of her medical bag. She turned to Old Suzy. "I'll be back on Thursday to check on the whooping cough. Keep a close eye on Henry, and keep him quiet as you can." She paused. "And if you could get his mother to unbar the cabin window, some fresh air and sunlight could get in. All that smoke and damp just aggravates the cough."

Old Suzy didn't say anything. I had heard that the people believed closed shutters kept evil influences away from the sick.

"All right." Laura Towne sighed resignedly. "I'll leave everything in your hands until Thursday. Send word if you need me sooner."

We climbed into the carriage, and Miss Towne picked up the reins. "By the way, Suzy, what's this I hear about some of the people wishing their old masters would come back?"

If Laura Towne meant this as a teasing remark, Suzy did not respond to it lightly. She drew herself up, and a look of supreme contempt came on her withered features.

"Dat's cuz dey's got no sense den, miss," she said shortly. "We don't want Secesh. No *indeed,* miss, no indeed, dey treat we too bad. Dey tuk ebery one my chilen away from me. When we sick and c'ldn't work dey tuk away all our food; gib us nutten to eat. Dey's orful hard, miss."

"I hope they don't come back then, Suzy," Miss Towne assured her gently, her tone penitent. "I think we're all gettting along fine without them." She started the horse with a flick of the reins, and we both waved good-bye to Suzy and the several heads that appeared in doorways at the sound of carriage wheels starting up.

"I shudder to think what will happen to these people if the South wins the war," Miss Towne said as we trotted along the pleasant road home. "They've had a taste of freedom now. They could never bear slavery again."

Since most of the news we had heard all autumn long had been of Northern defeats, it was hard to keep back pessimism. The single exception to the long series of losses suffered by the Union armies had been McClellan's victory over General Lee at Antietam, Maryland, on September 17. President Lincoln had taken advantage of that success to announce that on the coming New Year's Day he would issue an emancipation proclamation freeing the slaves in all the rebellious states. The announcement had brought great joy to radical Republicans and antislavery people, though one could have wished that Lincoln was not still trying to placate the border states—Kentucky, West Virginia, Missouri, Maryland, and Delaware—by exempting their slaves from the proclamation.

Since Antietam, things had not gone well for the Union armies. McClellan was dilly-dallying overcautiously on the northern bank of the Potomac, allowing Lee to outmaneuver him and edge closer to Washington. In Kentucky General Buell had likewise hesitated to press his advantage against the Confederate army, and Lincoln had been forced to replace him with a general who proved even less competent. Only in the west, along the Mississippi where General Ulysses S. Grant commanded the Army of the Tennessee, did things look hopeful. After a sickening defeat at Shiloh, Tennessee, Grant was maneuvering well to gain control of the entire Mississippi River, a campaign in which he would eventually succeed after laying siege to Vicksburg. But meanwhile one heard reports of Grant's terrible drunkenness, which scarcely inspired faith in his abilities. News reached us irregularly at Port Royal, and it was hard even then to separate fact from rumor, so we had limited knowledge of the state of the war, and this only added to our anxiety.

I felt very glum and must have looked it, for Laura Towne suddenly laughed gaily at me. "Just think, Charlotte, here we are—a couple of women deep within Confederate lines, danger on all sides, doing our best to cure an outbreak of whooping cough among the freedmen. It's really quite funny when you stop to think about it."

I had to agree, and joined her in laughing at myself, an art at which I've never been accomplished enough.

"I only hope it all comes true though," I added seriously a few moments later. "Emancipation, I mean. That copy of the *Liberator* that found me the other day says there are rumors that Lincoln may change his mind. He's fussing about compensating the Southern states for their slaves, and he's looking again at old colonization schemes. Basically he's so terribly conservative about the whole idea that it scares me."

"I've heard it said by those who admire Lincoln that he's slow to come to a decision, but once he's made up his mind he rarely changes it," Miss Towne said. "I think we'll have an emancipation proclamation, but I hope and pray we win this awful war, so that it's a lasting emancipation. Meanwhile I guess the best we can do is to go on living day by day, helping the slaves who have already been freed right here on St. Helena. At least that's my intention."

My admiration for Miss Towne reached new heights during that drive, and I took inspiration from her calm courage in the midst of such uncertainty. It was not many days later that we had encouraging news from our own General Saxton about the plans for emancipation.

The occasion was Thanksgiving Day, November 27, 1862. The day dawned cool and clear with delicious

air, golden, gladdening sunlight, and soft white clouds
afloat in a deep blue sky. Most of my life's Thanksgiv-
ings had occurred in cold, gray, tree-bare settings,
complete sometimes with snow, so I took special delight all the way to church in the blooming oleanders,
japonicas, and roses, the ripening figs and oranges, the
warmth and balminess of the air.

General Saxton had declared the day a general holiday, and the people entered into its spirit with relish.
An ox had been killed on each plantation and was
roasting for the feast that would come later in the day
and would provide rare and welcome fresh meat for us
all. The people had garbed themselves in their brightest, gayest finery—even brighter and gayer than their
usual Sunday costume. Freedmen, superintendents,
and teachers crowded in great numbers into the little
Baptist Church to hear their favorite, "Gen'l Saxby."

The church looked beautiful, if I do say so. Miss
Murray and I had decorated it the day before with
bright leaves and berries. The Reverend Samuel Phillips, our excellent but boring preacher, looked like a
veritable Pan rising behind his vine-bedecked pulpit.
He began the service with prayers and a typical dry
sermon. Hymns and spirituals followed. The spirituals
were rendered with far more gusto than the hymns, for
the island people were still unfamiliar with the melodies in the hymnbook. Then General Saxton stood to
speak to the black people. Sun streaming through the
east window made highlights on the braid of his epau-
lettes, on his metal buttons, on belt buckle and sword,
so that this distinguished-looking man drew a mo-

ment's murmur of admiration. In a short, spirited speech he talked of the volunteer regiment he was forming at Beaufort, a regiment that would be called the First South Carolina Volunteers and would be the first all-Negro regiment in the country. Commanding the regiment, he announced, was a man who had just arrived from the North and who had stood up for the black man time and time again. He had risked physical danger and imprisonment to help fugitive slaves and would see that no wrong ever came to the freedmen of St. Helena. The man was Colonel Thomas Wentworth Higginson.

If the name meant little to the island people, it pleased me immensely. I remembered the role Higginson had played in the Anthony Burns affair. And only last summer I had seen him smartly drilling a company of the Fifty-first Massachusetts Volunteers in the streets of Worcester. To think that he was here at Port Royal! The freedmen could have no finer, more sympathetic commander than he.

General Saxton went on to talk about a local hero well known to his audience. Robert Smalls was a slave who had grown up in Beaufort and become pilot of a Confederate steamer, the *Planter*. The *Planter* was at sea at the time of "gun shoot," so Smalls had not been freed, but from that moment he watched for an opportunity to escape from the Secesh. One night during the past May the *Planter* had been anchored in Charleston Harbor, and the ship's officer went ashore. Smalls seized his opportunity. He raised anchor and ran the Confederate flag up the masthead; then he navigated the boat with its crew of forty-five slaves out of Charleston Harbor. Once on the open ocean he exchanged the Confederate colors for a Union flag and took the steamer down the coast to Beaufort, where he surrendered it to the Union army. Small's daring maneuver was lauded by Negroes and white soldiers alike. Since the event, Smalls had been operating a small freedmen's store in Beaufort and was prospering nicely. Now General Saxton announced to the Thanksgiving congregation that Robert Smalls had come to see him only that morning, eager to enlist in the new regiment.

"Although he is earning fifty dollars a week in his store, he is giving it up to become a private in the First South Carolina Volunteers. Can you imagine why?" General Saxton looked about the room. "Robert told me only a few hours ago, 'How can I expect to keep my freedom if I'm not willing to fight for it? Suppose the Secesh should come back? What good would my fifty dollars a week do me then? Yes sir, I'd enlist if I were making a thousand dollars a week!' "

Though General Saxton didn't attempt to imitate Small's manner of speaking, the black hero's message came through sincerely. A buzz of talk swept the congregation until the general resumed.

"You have heard about the Emancipation Proclamation. It will soon announce to the world your freedom and the freedom of other slaves throughout the South. It will be a day of jubilation, and I invite you all to come to the army camp at Beaufort to help us celebrate the great event. I hope before that, however, that many of you young men will enlist in our regiment and encourage your friends to enlist too, so you can march on the day of celebration. The black troops I've had in my command since I arrived in July have done commendably. Two expeditions have gone out this month to fight rebel strongholds in Georgia and Florida, and both have returned victorious. Not only did the soldiers fight well, but they brought back captured stores and freed slaves. I am proud of what my men have done. I am proud that they understand the need to fight to make sure of lasting freedom. I would be proud if many hundreds more joined our regiment and our great cause."

I had the sense the general's plea was well received by the black men of St. Helena. Their faith in "Gen'l Saxby" could wipe away much of the distrust General Hunter had created a few months earlier.

After the service six couples were married, as frequently happened on Sunday. It was delightful to see the pride and happiness of the young participants, who were ingeniously decked out in such bridal finery as could be procured or manufactured from curtain laces and abandoned Secesh garments.

Slave marriages had formerly been treated as casual affairs. All that was needed to marry was the master's permission. The master might say a blessing over the heads of the plighted couple, but more often the marriage was considered done if the bride and groom just stepped over the handle of a broom in the presence of other slaves. Slave marriages never, before the coming of Northerners, took place in church, nor were they binding either legally or morally or in the eyes of the owner. A slaveholder could end the union simply by selling one slave.

Part of our mission at Port Royal was to help the freedmen develop a sense of family pride and unity that had been lacking under slavery. Church marriages performed in the sight of God and the presence of witnesses strengthened the marriage union, and the freedmen accepted this long withheld privilege so enthusiastically that several old couples, long wed, came to be married again with Christian ceremony. We also encouraged families to eat together at table, a novel experience for ex-slaves who had taken their meals wherever there was opportunity—in the field, in the sawmill, in the kitchen of the main house—while young children were fed from a trough by whomever was in charge of them.

Since "gun shoot," responsibility within the freedmen's families had shifted. Under slavery women had dominated. They cared for the cabin, bore and disciplined the children, who were thereafter considered the mother's property rather than the father's. On most plantations women went after the weekly and monthly rations meted out by the overseer. Women ground the family supply of corn and prepared the food; women received the ration of cloth and manufactured the necessary garments. With freedom, however, the men of the islands became the wage earners and decision makers, the soldiers and community leaders, the ones to whom the new superintendents turned. As a result the father had assumed the position of family head, and we hoped that this more natural state of affairs would persist.

The weeks between Thanksgiving and Christmas slipped by with lovely weather throughout. At night the temperature dropped, so that occasionally in the morning we found thin ice skimming our wash basins, but the days were quickly warmed by bright sunlight, and we often conducted school out of doors. Imagine a schoolroom with soft brown earth for carpet, blue sky for ceiling, and grand old oaks bedecked with moss draperies for walls, and you see the pleasantest setting in which teacher and pupils ever had lessons.

Not long before Christmas I received a letter from John Greenleaf Whittier in which he sent a beautiful hymn written especially for the children of St. Helena to sing on Emancipation Day. I commenced teaching it to the children at once, showing them Whittier's photograph and telling them what a friend the Quaker poet had long been to the blacks. Within a few days the sweet, true voices of my students were blended in new song.

> Oh, none in all the world before
>   Were ever glad as we!
> We're free on Carolina's shore,
>   We're all at home and free.
>
> We hear no more the driver's horn
>   No more the whip we fear,
> This holy day that saw Thee born
>   Was never half so dear.

> The very oaks are greener clad,
>   The waters brighter smile;
> Oh, never shone a day so glad
>   On sweet St. Helen's Isle.
>
> Come once again, O blessed Lord!
>   Come walking on the sea!
> And let the mainlands hear the word
>   That set the islands free!

Christmas was a happy occasion, although but prelude to the great day anticipated a week later. Miss Towne, Miss Murray, and I decorated our school with holly and cassena berries, with moss festoons and evergreen wreaths. Lizzie and I worked late Christmas Eve, finishing little aprons for the Oaklands children, and we were wakened early Christmas morning by the people knocking at our window and calling, "Merry Christmas." After breakfast we distributed bright red dresses to the babies on our plantation, aprons and oranges to the older children, and apple pies to the grown-ups. At school still more presents were given out to delighted, excited students—bright material for shirts and pantaloons or for dresses for the boys and girls, little bags of sewing utensils for the older girls. The children sang and sang, and all the people spent a good part of the day in impromptu shouts, held wherever groups happened to gather.

It was very different from any earlier Christmas, and I must admit to the most severe bout of homesickness I had known since being in the South. For myself a single letter from dear friends up North would have seemed a bountiful Christmas gift, but none appeared. Yet one bit of good news came to me that day. My old friend Dr. Seth Rogers, who a year earlier had helped me through a time of physical and spiritual illness at his water cure in Worcester, was to arrive at Port Royal to be surgeon to the new Negro regiment at Camp Saxton. I could expect to see him there on Emancipation Day!

That New Year's Eve a full moon cast light down on the camp of the First South Carolina Volunteers, located just west of Beaufort, South Carolina. The scene was already well illuminated from below by a great pit filled with flame, over which hung the carcasses of ten oxen. Tending the fire and revolving the large spits were several dozen happy soldiers, blacks all, who had been granted permission to stay up through the night to roast meat for next day's emancipation feast.

Whenever he awoke in his tent that night, the young colonel of the regiment, Thomas Wentworth Higginson, could hear his men chattering and laughing. He could smell the cooking meat and could glimpse glimmering flames that threw fantastic shadows among the oaks. He could smile to himself about his calm orders to the quartermaster that morning to slaughter ten beasts for the occasion, he who in private life had never ordered a beef roast larger than three pounds. How long the meat should cook he would leave to his merry soldiers, for this and the knowledge of how many gallons of molasses, vinegar, and ginger added to a barrel of water would produce tomorrow's beverage were beyond his ken.

By ten o'clock on New Year's morning, visitors began arriving at Camp Saxton by land and sea. I myself had risen unusually early and, with Lizzie and Mr. Hunn, had been carted in a borrowed carriage behind a remarkably slow horse to St. Helena ferry. There we boarded the *Flora,* on which a band loaned for the day by the Eighth Maine played gay airs for us all the way to Camp Saxton. An eager, wondering crowd of freed people was aboard, dressed in holiday attire, with the gayest of head handkerchiefs, the whitest of aprons, and the happiest of faces. The band was playing, the flags flying, everybody talking excitedly and feeling strangely happy.

Just as my foot touched the plank on landing, a hand grasped mine and a familiar voice said, "Charlotte!" There was dear, noble Dr. Rogers. What a joy it was to see a friend, and such a friend, from the North. We shook hands warmly and eagerly asked each other a dozen questions to catch up on news of the past year. Then, tucking my hand into his arm, Dr. Rogers took me on a tour of the camp, both of us chattering all the way.

Camp Saxton was situated on the site of an old seventeenth-century Huguenot fort. The doctor had appropriated a fairly recent structure, a gin house, to convert into the camp hospital. He proudly showed me his ten beds with straw pallets, his surgery and kitchen. All the doctor needed was a patient or two to begin his duties as regimental doctor.

As time neared for the official ceremony to begin, we followed the crowds to a beautiful big oak grove in which a platform had been erected for speakers, band, and guests. I was shown to a seat among the ladies and had several minutes in which to admire the black soldiers sitting and standing in their blue coats and scarlet trousers. Crowds of onlookers, superintendents, teachers, officers and cavalry men, and of course the freedmen, men, women and children, were grouped under the trees, their faces wearing a happy, expectant look. Beyond the people I could glimpse the blue river sparkling in the sun.

General Saxton had planned the ceremonies with loving care, from the opening prayer by the regiment chaplain to the final lusty singing of "John Brown's Body" by the soldiers. Included were several stirring speeches and the reading of the Emancipation Proclamation. But the most moving moment of all was quite unplanned. After the reading of the Emancipation Proclamation, Colonel Higginson stood to receive the colors. At the sight of the unfurled American flag and the handsome new regimental flag, a strong but quavering male voice near the platform suddenly broke into "My country, 'tis of thee, Sweet land of liberty, Of thee I sing." His was joined by feminine voices, and shortly all the black people sitting and standing throughout the grove were singing verse after verse of the hymn. As Colonel Higginson said later, the event was as natural and irrepressible as the morning note of the song sparrow, and it brought tears to many eyes.

When the last strains had died away, Colonel Higginson, visibly moved, thanked the people for their great, unselfconscious tribute to the day of jubilee. Then he presented the flags to two Negro officers, Sergeant Prince Rivers and Corporal Robert Sutton, the color guard. Both spoke briefly before bearing the colors proudly away.

After the ceremony soldiers and guests alike went off to indulge their appetites on beef and molasses. The Hunns and I were led by Dr. Rogers to Colonel Higginson's table for a sumptuous and merry dinner. The colonel was absent, for he ate that day with his soldiers, but the rest of us talked and laughed and feasted in great high spirits.

Highlight of the afternoon was the dress parade. Because the ranks of the regiment had swelled to full strength in the weeks since Thanksgiving, volunteers responding to the inspired leadership of General Saxton and Colonel Higginson, the drill was a splendid sight. I had never seen a dress parade before and was greatly exhilarated by the lines of dark-skinned men in their bright uniforms, bayonets gleaming in the sun, marching through a maze of patterns. Many white soldiers along the sidelines—visitors from the camp at Hilton Head—professed themselves impressed by the discipline the black troops had learned so rapidly.

Later, when a group of us had the honor of visiting with Colonel Higginson in his tent, I commented upon the proficiency of his soldiers. The colonel agreed that the men drilled well, in fact, seemed to show a natural talent for marching.

"I've trained white companies with far more difficulty," Colonel Higginson told us. "To tell the truth, when I came down here, I was quite prepared for the worst. I believe that good discipline is the most important element of army training, and I thought I might have difficulty teaching drill and camp duty to troops so unused to the idea. On the contrary, it seems to me they learn far less laboriously than white soldiers. They almost never mistake left for right, and they're much more sedate and grave during instruction time than white troops are."

"I suppose some people would say that's because of the docility bred into them as slaves?" I ventured.

"Perhaps," he answered. "But they're not docile in spirit. They just seem to separate the extremes of jollity and sobriety more than white soldiers. When they're drilling, they're all business. The moment they're dismissed from drill every tongue is wagging, and they're dancing and shouting, 'Ki! Ole man,' at each other."

As Colonel Higginson talked, I glanced about his tent which he had made comfortable with one or two homelike touches. A fine secretary stood against one canvas wall with writing utensils and a copy of *Les Misérables* displayed upon it. On another wall, opposite the door, hung a lovely wreath of bitter oranges. A bit of carpeting, a few daguerreotypes, and some chairs and stools completed the "parlor," cut off from the colonel's sleeping quarters by a curtain.

At last the day drew to a close. Reluctantly, for it would have been fun to stay for the grand shout the soldiers were planning that night, the Hunns and I wended our way to the landing. There we sat a while in soft, delicate moonlight among the ruins of the old fort to wait for the *Flora*. Moonlight reflected on the river, and somewhere a band was playing "Home, Sweet Home." I thought of friends up North and wondered how this glorious day had been celebrated there. Only later, as outdated newspapers trickled through to the Sea Islands, did I complete my picture of how the rest of the nation celebrated that eventful New Year's Day of 1863.

In Washington it was a gloomy, muddy day. The annual New Year's reception at the White House was held, despite dismal news of Union defeat in Tennessee where Rosecrans' Army of the Cumberland had been attacked by Southerners led by General Bragg. Toward the middle of the afternoon the tall, sad President entered his office, and with a right hand tired and swollen from hours of greeting callers, placed his full, trembling signature at the foot of the prosaic document lying on his desk. There was little ceremony. Fewer than a dozen cabinet members and officials, just those who happened to be at the White House at that hour, gathered round. At Lincoln's elbow stood Massachusetts Senator Charles Sumner. Sumner and Wendell Phillips had goaded—yea, hounded—Abraham Lincoln for over a year about issuing the Proclamation. Now it was done, in Lincoln's own time and in his own way. The word went out over the wires to the rest of the nation.

In Boston, center of the oldest and most radical antislavery fervor, a great crowd had gathered at the Music Hall to hear a concert and await news of the Proclamation, expected about noon. Henry Wadsworth Longfellow was there, and Whittier. Ralph Waldo Emerson was there, and Harriet Beecher Stowe. William Lloyd Garrison was there. The afternoon pulsed on, filled with orchestral strains, but no news. Had Lincoln changed his mind? The abolitionists were half ready to believe so. Then, when darkness had already begun to close down on the windy, snowy New England day, word came at last. The Proclamation was signed. At the Music Hall and in Tremont Temple, where another great gathering had waited patiently all day, bedlam broke out among the people. Shouting, hugging, kissing, waving of hats and handkerchiefs, could scarcely express the joy. In the balcony Mrs. Stowe dabbed at the tears streaming from her eyes and bowed to the crowds who called her name from below. Garrison, also the center of acclaim, stood silent, slowly realizing the crowning moment of his thirty-two–year campaign. On the Boston Common and in cities throughout the North, bells tolled and cannons belched forth salute.

And far to the South I sat in a rowboat, listening to the solemn, sonorous songs of free Negro boatmen who rowed us through the night toward our dark landing. The day of Negro emancipation, to which I had looked forward all my life, had come at last. What vast changes lay ahead for Negroes and for the nation were hard to imagine.

Chapter 6

~.·

The noise that had wakened me from a sound sleep was repeated. Someone was quietly trying to open my bedroom door. It was too dark to see the door handle, but I had no doubt that it was moving, for the sound at the latch was unmistakable. At once I was wide awake. I held my breath, listening intently. The door was locked, yet whoever was outside tried the handle a third time.

"Who's there?" I called loudly. Now the revolver that lay on the night table was in my hand, and I was sitting bolt upright, my stomach awash with fright. There was no answer.

I hadn't the courage to unlock the door. But I threw off my blanket and crept through the dark to the ad-

joining room where Miss Ware, a resident of the plantation I was visiting, lay peacefully asleep.

She awoke, bewildered, and managed to light her
candle and find her revolver. She followed me back to
my bed, and there we propped ourselves up, with
blankets drawn around our shoulders and guns
pointed at the door, ready for any intruder. There was
only one to be feared. The people never came near the
house at night, and burglars were unknown. But it
might, at last, be a rebel. Rumors of rebel attacks were
rife, and just that evening I had returned from a visit
to the headquarters of the First South Carolina Volunteers, stationed on picket duty at Port Royal Ferry
along the Coosaw River, where I had witnessed an exchange of shells between the Union soldiers and the
rebels. Perhaps the rebels had crossed the river and
broken through the picket lines. They could easily
have gotten to St. Helena and The Oaks, where I was
spending the night. It was no wild supposition.

And what would the rebels do to us? We had heard
of their vengeance sworn against the Northern superintendents and teachers who were shepherding the Sea
Islands' ten thousand freedmen and occupying former
Southern homes. We could prepare for the worst.

Our door was not touched again. Miss Ware and I
sat in our defiant postures for over an hour, weapons
pointed toward the door, until we grew intolerably
sleepy. When our candle neared its end, so did our
vigil, and we woke later in broad daylight to find we
had slept soundly, wrapped in our blanket shrouds.

There was no explanation for my midnight caller,

for the rebels had not crossed the river and no one else had been alarmed in the night. The incident was merely one of many that kept us alert to the possible dangers surrounding us. While at times I might be seduced by the narcissus and japonicas, the jessamine and roses, the beautiful peach blossoms and fragrant orange blossoms, into believing I trod in paradise, the war went on, and we were regularly and frequently reminded that men were fighting and dying not far away.

During January of 1863 the First South Carolina Regiment had seen its first action during an expedition up the St. Mary's River, the stream that formed the boundary between Georgia and Florida. Colonel Higginson announced modestly that he was taking his men off on a foraging expedition, a trip to capture some badly needed brick and lumber supplies known to be cached at mills along the river. But everyone knew it was more than that. For the first time an all-Negro regiment was going on wartime maneuvers. The black soldiers would be tested. Would they prove disciplined and courageous under gunfire? Colonel Higginson had no doubts, but he knew that the actions of his regiment would be carefully scrutinized by many in the North who were skeptical of how Negroes would stand up to danger.

Above all the black men he commanded, Thomas Wentworth Higginson admired his young corporal, Robert Sutton, a large, powerful man whom Higginson called the natural prime minister of his troops. Sutton was untutored, yet was a man of superior intellect who reasoned systematically and comprehensively and who grasped military problems with a vigor that greatly impressed his commanding officer. Sutton had escaped in a dugout from a plantation on the St. Mary's River, and it was his information about supplies to be procured along that waterway that inspired Higginson to undertake the expedition.

Later I heard in detail about the regiment's exploits, for my friend Dr. Seth Rogers kept meticulous notes which he read to me on his return, and the soldiers themselves came back with enthusiastic accounts of their adventures. After steaming down the coast in three large boats, the regiment landed a few miles up the St. Mary's and marched by night on a camp of rebel cavalry. The ensuing battle proved that a lot of nonsense had been written about the valor of colored troops under fire. The men neither flinched nor fled, and bore their first wounds with a degree of pride. Three nights later Higginson organized his small fleet to ascend the St. Mary's still farther. Two hundred soldiers packed into the hold of the *John Adams,* an old East Boston double-ender ferry boat which had been transformed into an army gunboat. With its great sidewheel, originally designed to break through ice, the *John Adams* drew seven feet of water. It was an ideal boat in which to mount the river on the rising tide. The captain of the *John Adams,* a civilian, was assisted in his piloting by Robert Sutton, who knew the intricacies of the stream. Without Sutton's guidance the expedition would have been impossible. As it was, the boat was obliged at the sharpest turns in the river to run straight aground, let the tide carry its other end up into the channel, and then reverse the motion. Considering that the riverbanks were heavily wooded, the maneuver was a tricky one. But the moon was full, the landscape silent, and for long stretches the *John Adams* ran smoothly upriver, bearing men whose senses were keenly alert to the dangers ahead. One hour before daybreak on January 30, 1863, the Union force dropped anchor at the little town of Woodstock, Florida. The soldiers quietly went ashore and surrounded the homes of the people living there.

The anticipated wealth of lumber was stacked at Woodstock, and not far away was a great supply of brick. The soldiers set to work loading both, and took a few of the Southern citizens on board the *John Adams* as hostages for the trip home. Costly furniture was discovered stored in buildings along the town's wharves. It had been sent upriver for safety from abandoned homes farther east along the St. Mary's. Higginson ordered that nothing was to be confiscated or burned, and presumably most householders along the river repossessed their furnishings after the war.

Corporal Sutton had been the slave of the wealthiest family in Woodstock. His former mistress still lived in a handsome house adjacent to her lumber mills, so Higginson and Sutton went calling on her. The Colonel thoroughly enjoyed the look of unutterable indignation that came over the Southern lady's face when Higginson reintroduced her to Robert Sutton. "Like so many drops of nitric acid," he described the words

that fell from her proud lips: "Yes," she said. *"We
called him Bob!"*

Perhaps in answer, Robert Sutton took Colonel Higginson to a small building not far from the main
house and flung open the door. On the door itself was
a large metal staple and great rusty chain. Here slaves
had been fastened for beating. Inside the slave-jail
were three sets of stocks, one with holes small enough
for children. The corner was occupied by a peculiar-
looking cage, designed so that a person imprisoned in
it could neither sit nor stand nor lie, but must support
himself in a very painful position. On the table lay an
assortment of whips and chains. Higginson was
tempted to burn the hateful structure to the ground,
but feared that every other building would go up in
smoke, taking the precious piles of lumber as well, so
he contented himself with locking the jail and carrying
off its keys.

Loaded with lumber, bricks, tools, forty bushels of
rice, and a large flock of sheep, the *John Adams* began
the drop downriver in broad daylight. This was the
riskiest part of the trip, for rebel cavalry had had time
to assemble and they began to harass the *John Adams*
from the many bluffs looking down on the river. For
several miles, as the Union boat twisted and turned in
the current, a rain of bullets swept down upon the vessel. The gun crews aboard the boat kept up a steady
shelling from three parrot guns and a howitzer
mounted on the deck. Higginson ordered most of his
soldiers to stay below, for their musketry was not effec-

tive under these circumstances. In the hold the men fought one another for the chance to take potshots from the portholes.

The boat ran a long gamut of gunfire, and though it could easily and successfully have been stopped short had the rebels just felled a tree or two at one of the narrow river bends, this did not happen. The rebels only galloped along the river from vantage point to vantage point, harassing the vessel. Though the pilot house of the *John Adams* was soon peppered with bullet holes, casualties were surprisingly light. The captain of the boat was killed, however, and Robert Sutton and the mate had to take over the piloting. They finally navigated the expedition safely to the mouth of the St. Mary's where the *John Adams* made rendezvous with its two companion ships. The First South Carolina Volunteers steamed up the coast to the Sea Islands, proud and victorious, every soldier eager to tell his version of the "expeditious."

Bigger maneuvers were in store for Colonel Higginson's troops, and amazingly enough, they involved me. One mid-February day as I was teaching my small charges at the brick church, who should appear at the schoolroom door but dear Dr. Rogers. In he came, and Miss Murray and I set the children to reading and singing for him. Seth Rogers was full of praise for their performance. The children grinned and squirmed with delight at his kind and well-deserved remarks.

Dr. Rogers accompanied me to Oaklands for dinner with the Hunns. Our menu was exceedingly limited those days, but Arametta did her best to suggest variety. Dr. Rogers complimented her upon her efforts and later thanked Cupid for his contribution of crabs, a welcome change from the impenetrable beef that was the steady camp ration.

After dinner I accompanied Dr. Rogers on a visit to a nearby plantation. Riding had become my chief form of recreation, and I had acquired a little Secesh pony. The Carolina horses, though smaller and more mean-looking than those in the North, were well trained and excellent for the saddle. We rode for miles each day through the beautiful pine barrens, which in February possessed the inebriating quality of a New England May. The peach and wild plum blossoms, the buzzing bees and trilling birds wooed our senses, while on the ground young ferns and lavender myrtle cushioned our step.

That day Seth Rogers and I found the trees trapped in great webs of jessamine, its fragrance and yellow brightness overwhelming the landscape. Dr. Rogers broke off several long, willowy sprays and twined them around me until I looked grand as a queen. How good Mr. Hunn opened his eyes when he saw me returning to Oaklands so gloriously adorned!

But Dr. Rogers' chief reason for coming to Oaklands was to bring me a note from Colonel Higginson relating a marvelous scheme. According to the letter, the First South Carolina Volunteers were awaiting orders to go to Florida, to take and hold the city of Jacksonville on the St. John's River. Jacksonville had been occupied and abandoned twice before by Union troops.

Now General Hunter, commander of the Department of the South, hoped that the local knowledge possessed by Higginson's black troops, a full company of whom came from Florida, would be useful in again securing the area and bringing Florida back into the Union. I was being asked to join the regiment, once Jacksonville was held, to set up a school in which the soldiers of the regiment could be taught to read and write. It was a scheme such as only Thomas Wentworth Higginson, with his broad concern for all aspects of the lives of his men, would have thought of. I was thrilled and flattered by the whole prospect.

The regiment would go by boat, probably during the first week in March, Dr. Rogers told me. When that happened, I was to talk with Laura Towne and Ellen Murray about leaving school, then await my orders to depart for Florida. Until instructed, I was to tell no one of the plan, for the regiment's movements must be kept secret. How I would keep the news to myself I knew not, for I was highly excited at the thought of being partner, in however small a way, to the dreams of Colonel Higginson for helping the freedmen prepare for their new role in American life. Through my mind flashed the memory of a time when I yearned to be useful to my race but knew not how. Now, on the verge of using my talents to capacity, I felt joyful and fulfilled.

The time between my ride with Dr. Rogers and the departure of the regiment passed swiftly enough. One day I spent at the headquarters of the regiment, hearing from Colonel Higginson's own lips his plan for me to go to Florida. How deep was his interest in the black people! After talking over the Florida venture, we discussed our mutual interest in the freedmen's hymns. Colonel Higginson confessed himself as enchanted as I by the originality and beauty of the songs. When I mentioned my concern that our Northern melodies might begin replacing the native ones, so that eventually some of the spirituals would be lost, I discovered that Colonel Higginson had been doing what I was doing, recording the songs he heard sung at shouts and around the campfires and on marches. I promised to copy for him the spirituals I had written down and the songs I knew Miss Murray had recorded.

But Colonel Higginson was greatly preoccupied that day by a matter more urgent than spirituals. He had just heard that the government was going back on its promise to pay the black soldiers the same wages paid to white soldiers, and the news made him highly indignant.

"I gave the men my word, Miss Forten. I gave them my word that they would receive thirteen dollars a month just like every other soldier in the Union army! The written pledge of the War Department to General Saxton states the matter clearly! But now it seems Congress finds black troops are worth only ten dollars a month, and they're even haggling over that." The colonel shook his head angrily.

"There's more than distress involved here," he went on. "Though goodness knows most of these soldiers are the sole support of their families, and they've scarcely enough to live on. But the fact is that the United

States government is being dishonest. It's saying to these freedmen, 'Your government hasn't sufficient integrity to fulfill an explicit business contract.' It's also saying, 'You may be free, but don't think you're equal. We'll pay your regiment's officers their full wages, but we won't pay you yours, and we won't let any black man be a commissioned officer either.' Do you wonder that these men question whether they're any better off today than they were under the Secesh? Why, all their friends who refused to join the regiment are laughing at them. They're adding to the humiliation by saying 'I told you so.' " The colonel's voice was wrathful.

"There's another problem, too," interjected John Hunn, who had accompanied me to Camp Saxton. "You've heard about the new land-ownership plan that Richard Soule has put forward? The government will soon begin selling off parcels of the plantations to the freedmen, so that a system of private enterprise can get launched at Port Royal. Your soldiers, Colonel Higginson, won't have any money to buy land."

"The very land they're defending with their lives," I said, shocked that it could be so.

"That's right, Miss Forten, the very land they're willing to die for. That's the irony of the matter." Colonel Higginson was tight-lipped. "I've written to Washington, and General Saxton has appealed to the War Department. If we don't have good news soon I plan to begin a series of letters to the *New York Tribune*. Horace Greeley will be sympathetic, and he'll arouse some public interest in the matter.

So noble were his intentions, so zealous his commit-

ment to his soldiers, it seemed impossible that Thomas
Wentworth Higginson's views should not prevail. Yet
it was to be so. Years of effort to secure for his men the
full wages to which they were entitled would come to
naught.

On March 6, 1863, the regiment broke camp and
departed for Florida. Next day I talked with Misses
Towne and Murray about leaving our school. They
were reluctant to part with me but generously recognized my greater opportunity to help the freedmen, so
gave me their blessing.

One of the days while I yet lingered at Port Royal,
Lizzie Hunn and I made a trip to Beaufort to shop and
to pay a visit to a wonderful Negro woman named
Harriet Tubman. We had learned from the people of
her presence in Beaufort just about the same time an
article in the *Liberator* called our attention to it. I
greatly desired before leaving the Sea Islands to shake
the hand of this wonderful woman, who was called
Moses by the people. A deliverer she truly was, for
over the past two decades she alone had helped nearly
two hundred slaves escape from the South. Born a
slave in Maryland, Harriet Tubman had escaped after
being abused by her master and abandoned by her
husband. There was said to be a reward of ten thousand dollars upon her head, yet she fearlessly returned
again and again into the South to help fugitives make
their way north.

We found Harriet Tubman in the kitchen of an eating house she was running in Beaufort. It was a temporary occupation, the short, amazingly ugly woman in

apron and head handkerchief told us cheerfully. "I want to go back north as soon as I can manage it," she explained. "There's lots of folks helping the black man here. But there's freedmen up north who are having a mighty difficult time."

Harriet Tubman had us sit down in chairs on her little porch and settled herself into a rocker. Beneath her skirts I could see feet clad in men's worn work boots, and fleetingly I thought of the many hundreds of miles those feet must have walked over the past few years. Harriet Tubman was a master storyteller, and she had thrilling tales to relate. We sat spellbound as she narrated some of her exploits, holding our breaths as she hid with escaped slaves in the woods by day, weeping tears of joy as she jubilantly described bringing her fugitives to their final refuge. How I admired this heroic woman! How glad I was to have shaken her hand!

On the twenty-fourth of March my orders came from Florida. I was to sail from Hilton Head two days hence in the company of General Saxton! My excitement knew no bounds. Tucked into the letter from Colonel Higginson was a note from Dr. Rogers. "We have to keep a sharp outlook for the rebels, but I think we shall hold the town," he had jotted. Far from frightening me, the prospect of danger added spice to the whole adventure.

With full heart I said good-bye next day to my scholars at the brick church. As parting gift I gave them each a little book. They seemed delighted. Laura Towne stopped at Oaklands that afternoon to help me

pack my trunk. She brought with her Mr. Edward
Pierce, the original organizer of the Port Royal experiment, who had just returned to the Sea Islands from
Boston and who planned to take passage on my boat to
Florida. How refreshing it was to talk with someone
full of Boston energy and spirit. All that prevented me
from liking Mr. Pierce immediately was the nagging
memory of a remark he was supposed to have made,
that he wanted no "colored missionaries nor teachers
down here." I planned to get to the bottom of that
speech before counting him my friend.

Miss Towne and Mr. Pierce went on to The Oaks. I
followed with Cupid after tea, saying good-bye to the
island as we drove along. St. Helena looked so beautiful in the still, late light. I hated to think I might
never see it or any of the inhabitants again. So verging
on sadness was I that if Cupid had felt talkative, he
would have been answered by yards of tears from me.
But he said little.

Next morning we rose early—Laura Towne, Mr.
Pierce, and I—and we were early at the ferry. Despite
it, the boat was already halfway across the river on its
first run to Beaufort, and we had to sit on our trunks
at the landing and wait for it to return. We talked, and
Mr. Pierce read passages from a newly published book
called *My Diary North and South* by a correspondent
for the *London Times*. After a while we noticed the
Flora going down the river, carrying General Saxton. I
began to worry that the ship might depart from Hilton
Head without us, but Mr. Pierce was more calm. At
last the ferry returned and carried us to Beaufort. We

went at once to Captain Hooper's office to discover what boat would carry us to Hilton Head, and there learned some distressing news. Word had come that General Hunter was ordering the evacuation of Jacksonville. General Saxton had gone downriver to consult with him about it. My hopes fell in a heap inside me. Could it be true? Could we not be going to Florida after all?

"The vagaries of war," Mr. Pierce called it, shrugging his shoulders. "Now, Charlotte, you know what soldiers go through," he said with a wry smile. "March here one minute, march back again the next. General Saxton is expected right back, and we'll just have to wait for him before we know what's going on."

We waited. We dined with friends in Beaufort. At last General Saxton arrived, and we learned that the story was true. General Hunter was planning an expedition against Charleston, where the rebels had been gathering in great force. He needed all troops available to mount the offensive and couldn't spare enough men to support Colonel Higginson's First South Carolina Volunteers as they should be supported if Jacksonville was to be successfully held. The Florida campaign would have to be launched again, after Charleston was taken.

I can't tell you how dismal it seemed to row back across the Beaufort River to the island I had so fondly yet happily abandoned a few hours earlier. Nor how dreary it seemed to find myself back teaching school to my same small urchins with little hope that I would ever see Florida. Only the thought that I might still teach the soldiers when they returned to Port Royal sustained me. My spirits were so in revolt at the turn-about of events that I shortly succumbed to a cold, the worst I've ever had, and spent over a week quite stupe-fied with its symptoms and with excessive doses of cam-omile tea.

The only good part of the aftermath of my disap-pointment was that I came to know Edward Pierce very well, for he stayed on at The Oaks and frequently came calling at Oaklands. One day as we sat before one of Cupid's fires, fending off the chill wind that blew a raw, disagreeable day right into the sitting room through the cracks in the floor, I asked him about the prejudicial remark I had heard attributed to him. He emphatically denied having made it, and the long talk we had together concerning prejudice took down the bars of formality between us and convinced me that there was only good in this man. From that moment we were friends, and many were the conversations we held about antislavery efforts and about his friendship with the noble Charles Sumner. I never tired of hear-ing Edward Pierce reminisce about Sumner, nor did Mr. Pierce ever seem to run out of stories to tell.

The regiment came home, every soldier even more disappointed about the recall than I had been. The general feeling among the men was that the regiment could have held Jacksonville against quite a force of rebels had it been allowed to stay. The South Carolina troops had driven the enemy back from the city and had burned the railroad for several miles. It was hard to leave what seemed a secure position. Shortly, however, the men forgot their disappointment. Attention began to focus on Charleston and on the expedition that was mounting against that rebel stronghold.

The weather grew steadily warmer. Colonel Higginson's regiment was sent out on picket along the Coosaw River, a maneuver that had all the makings of a military picnic. Interspersed with small skirmishes with the enemy were opportunities to gather oysters and pick blackberries, as well as to take horseback rides along lanes lined with wild roses and magnolias and carpeted with sand violets. The colored soldiers, with their love of country life and pleasure in visiting other plantations, looked on picket duty as a festival.

During April fortifications were constructed around Beaufort. These reminded us that warfare was imminent, yet somehow visions of fighting and dying did not seem real. As the weather grew hot, the Northerners on the islands sought escape from the discomfort of soaring temperatures and invading insects. It was the beginning of the fever season, the time of the year when the Secesh used to abandon their plantations to seek higher ground and sea breezes, away from the swamps and the insects that dwelt therein. The Hunns and I searched out a more refreshing location on the island. In May we moved to Seaside, an elegant old plantation on the other side of St. Helena, which at high tide overlooked the water but at low tide faced a vast marsh. Seaside felt healthier than Oaklands, for in the evenings it enjoyed a steady sea breeze. We adapted ourselves readily to the new household, which had two great advantages. First, Seaside boasted a piano! It was not the finest specimen of its kind, but there it stood, having miraculously escaped confiscation, and I took to practicing daily.

In addition, Seaside had a praise house. There were about one hundred people on the plantation, and several times a week they gathered for praise meetings and shouts. Here it was that old blind Maurice held forth triumphantly, and I think the scene at Judgment Day shall not surpass his ecstatic singing:

De talles' tree in Paradise
De Christian calls de Tree ob Life,
An' I hope dat trumpet blow me home
To my New Jerusalem.

(chorus)

Blow, Gabriel! trumpet, blow louder, louder!
An' I hope dat trumpet blow me home
To my New Jerusalem.

Paul and Silas jail-bound
Sing God's praise both night and day,
An' I hope dat trumpet blow me home
To my New Jerusalem!

(chorus)

Blow, Gabriel! trumpet, blow louder, louder!
An' I hope dat trumpet blow me home
To my New Jerusalem.

For diversion we continued to ride horseback, choosing the cool early morning or dusk for our excur-

sions to all parts of the island. Midday was too hot to
be in the saddle, but Cupid had found me an old sulky
to use. The rig was very tall. Indeed, mounting it was
no easy task, and when Laura Towne had provided a
shade of black India-rubber cloth, it looked like the
skeleton of same strange, prehistoric creature sur-
mounted by a huge bonnet. Driving about in it, I provided endless amusement for the people, especially the
soldiers who dubbed it "the calithumpian" and greeted
my appearance with shouts of laughter.

Several of the officers of the First South Carolina
Volunteers had by this time sent for their wives. The
quartermaster even imported his baby daughter! The
presence of ladies at camp headquarters was excuse for
social doings not ordinarily connected with a military
outpost. There was lots of visiting back and forth between the plantations and Camp Saxton, and when the
soldiers were on picket duty at Port Royal Ferry, we
followed the regiment to the Milne plantation, which
served as headquarters for Colonel Higginson and his
staff. Occasional excursions among the islands and exploring parties up the many rivers to abandoned plantations provided welcome change from the ongoing
tasks of teaching and farming and soldiering. Yet it
was this innocent gadding about that led to the dashing of my hopes for teaching the black soldiers at Port
Royal. Colonel Higginson, of course, approved the
plan wholeheartedly, but he hesitated when he learned
that rumors of scandal were circulating in the North.
Perhaps the presence of ladies was bound to create
such problems, for Northern females must have looked

with some envy upon the gay times reported from the Sea Islands. Yet I was annoyed and unhappy that I should be prevented from doing what I most desired because of common gossip. I appreciated Colonel Higginson's position and suffered his decision that I bide my time. Higginson knew the eyes of the nation were on his regiment and that many of those eyes were unfriendly and looked only for the opportunity to criticize the freedmen. For a while at least, he must be cautious.

The heat grew intense. Day after day during June I drove home from school thoroughly exhausted, to fall into bed until dark. In the evenings we would sit up late on the big piazza, enjoying the steady wind off the ocean and conversing about the war and the future with various visitors who came to the islands. At a certain hour the fleas would "rise" and drive us indoors. But the fleas were everywhere—in our beds, most of all—and the tortures we suffered from these minute tyrants made unbroken sleep a luxury. I became tired and then ill, and during the last of June was frequently absent from school.

Early in June a new black regiment had arrived in Port Royal. Almost immediately it left for an expedition on the Georgia coast, but it returned to St. Helena late in the month in preparation for the attack on Charleston. This was the Fifty-fourth Massachusetts Volunteers, the first Negro regiment to be recruited in the Northeast. Its officers and soldiers came from several states, for Massachusetts alone was not able to supply enough colored men to fill its ranks. The fact that the regiment existed at all was testimony to the desperation of the Union army. Like Higginson's regiment, it had come into being after Congress, in the face of continuing defeat and a scarcity of volunteers among white men, found it necessary to rule that black men could be armed. There was widespread ridicule of the idea in the North; there was also fear. The general sentiment of Northerners was that the Negro would not fight, and that even if he did, the war would be only unnecessarily prolonged. Besides, white soldiers would refuse to cooperate with black soldiers; they would balk against fighting next to them. The whole idea was considered a bad one, looked upon with deep suspicion.

Yet Governor John Andrew of Massachusetts did not think it an impossible scheme. He was an abolitionist; he had firm faith in what the Negro could achieve if given the opportunity, and forming a black regiment was such an opportunity. If he could find officers with ideals as high as his own to command the regiment, Andrew felt he could prove something to the country. He had several young men in mind. In January 1863 he wrote to Robert Gould Shaw, a captain in the Second Massachusetts Infantry, saying he was seeking to command the Negro regiment a man of strong antislavery principles, who was contemptuous of prejudice and who had faith in the capacity of black men for military service. Shaw was such a man. He accepted the colonelcy of the regiment. Two of the Hallowell brothers of Philadelphia agreed to be its lieutenant colonel and its major. A dozen other white men volunteered to leave their regiments to participate in the experiment.

It was not an easy decision for any of the officers, for this was no call to glory. William Simpkins, who left the Forty-fourth Massachusetts Infantry to become a captain in the Fifty-fourth, described wrestling over his decision.

"This is no hasty conclusion, no blind leap of an enthusiast, but the result of much hard thinking," he wrote. "It will not be at first, and probably not for a long time, an agreeable position, for many reasons too evident to state. . . . [It] is nothing but an experiment after all, but it is an experiment that I think it high time we should try,—an experiment which the sooner we prove fortunate the sooner we can count upon an immense number of hardy troops that can stand the effect of a southern climate without injury; an experiment which, the sooner we prove unsuccessful, the sooner we shall establish an important truth and rid ourselves of a false hope."

The experiment *was* to prove fortunate, for the Fifty-fourth quickly brought honor to itself and the black race. But for William Simpkins and many, many others, it was a fatal experiment, because by mid-summer they lay dead before the walls of Fort Wagner in Charleston Harbor.

The regiment was formed. Enlisting black soldiers were promised all the rights and privileges of white soldiers, that is, thirteen dollars a month and state aid for their families if needed. The first company came from Massachusetts. Company B was recruited in Philadelphia, the dear old City of Brotherly Love, where citizens kept up such harassment that the gathering place for the Fifty-fourth volunteers had to be kept secret, and enlisting soldiers were quietly sent off to Massachusetts by ones and twos, just as if they were fugitives. Company C was formed in New Bedford; Company D, in western Massachusetts and Connecticut; and the other six companies were recruited over a wide area from Buffalo west to St. Louis and in the rest of the New England States.

By May 12, 1863, the Fifty-fourth was a regiment of eight hundred soldiers, and on May 28 it marched proudly through Boston, past cheering crowds, to embark for the Sea Islands of South Carolina. Though the citizens of Boston applauded enthusiastically, people in other communities took a more jaundiced view of the Negro regiment. Many a Democratic editorial throughout the North scoffed as the Fifty-fourth set sail.

The regiment arrived at Hilton Head and camped with other regiments gathering under General George C. Strong on the southern end of St. Helena Island at a spot called Land's End. My first opportunity to meet Colonel Robert Gould Shaw came when he and Lieutenant Colonel Edward N. Hallowell, whom I knew from Philadelphia, spent an evening at Seaside in early July. They took tea with us and afterward witnessed their first shout. Old Maurice that night surpassed himself in singing and gesturing. The shout was one of the most spirited I ever attended, and our guests enjoyed it immensely. The weird, indescribable sadness in the minor-key melodies affected them as it did every Northerner who heard it.

I was charmed by Robert Gould Shaw. His youth, his fine-featured handsomeness, his graceful bearing and tender manner, were very appealing, and I could sense why his soldiers had quickly come to prize him so highly. He, in turn, was devoted to them. He praised the accomplishments that had rapidly turned some eight hundred free Northern Negro civilians into a group of disciplined soldiers. Shaw spoke openly of the coming attack on Charleston, expressing the hope that his men might be given a chance to prove themselves. "To do themselves honor" were his words as we sat on the piazza in the moonlight after the shout.

Edward Pierce, who was still with us, was a friend of Shaw's. He was also a friend to the Fifty-fourth, for back in February in Boston he had helped Governor Andrew and others recruit soldiers for the regiment, and he had since followed its activities closely. He was interested to know how the soldiers and officers had reacted to an act just passed by the Confederate Congress which threatened that any captured Negro soldier would be put to death or remanded to slavery and that any captured white officer who commanded black troops would be put to death or otherwise punished at the discretion of a Confederate court. This harsh law was directed at the several new Union Negro regiments that were being formed, and it violated the laws of warfare accepted by both North and South.

"All the venom in the Confederate breast inspired that act," Colonel Shaw replied quietly. "Southerners despise the Negro, and they despise any white man who associates with him. I think we all know what we face if we're captured. The men of the Fifty-fourth will be no ordinary prisoners of war."

His tone was gentle, so gentle that together with the moonlight and soft breeze and the overwhelming odor of oleander it reinforced the peaceful harmony of our surroundings. That Shaw spoke of war and killing seemed incongruous. For war even to be was impossible! Yet none of us would have been in this place otherwise. Ned Hallowell interrupted the pause by laughing.

"Our regiment appears to have put the rebels in a real quandary," he said good-humoredly. "After all, if they treated Negro prisoners of war like any other prisoners of war, they'd be treating them as equals, and that would be intolerable. So instead they'll treat them like escaped slaves, and either shoot them or send them back to their owners."

"But how many of them *are* fugitives?" I asked. "Aren't they all free men?"

"Not all," was Colonel Shaw's reply. "A few admit to having escaped. Most are free men though, and it will probably be worse for them when they're captured than it will for your contrabands of the First South Carolina Volunteers, because the owners of the contrabands can be found fairly easily. At least those soldiers won't be shot."

Courage is what it took to belong to the Fifty-fourth, I told my journal that night. Moral courage to take up an unpopular cause, and physical courage to see it through. Robert Gould Shaw and Ned Hallowell appeared to me to have plenty of both kinds.

Several days later a party of us rode to Land's End to watch a splendid dress parade and to be afterward entertained by the soldiers' singing. We remarked on the camaraderie evident among the men and officers of the Fifty-fourth and on the special pride the men seemed to take in their regiment. As we left, Colonel Shaw helped me onto my horse and kindly arranged the folds of my riding skirt. In the few moments of conversation we had together, he spoke of his parents and of the bride of a few weeks he had left in New York City. Since we did not realize departure of the regiment was imminent, we did not say farewell, but all in my party waved gaily and trotted off. Two days later, on July 8, 1863, the Fifty-fourth Massachusetts Volunteers left Port Royal, ordered north to Charleston. It was to be more than ten days before we had word of them, and then the story of what happened we learned bit by bit, piecing it together just as I later pieced together the shredded, mutilated clothing of some of the wounded survivors of that regiment. We heard the whole sad story, too, from the lips of Edward Pierce who was witness to the attack on Fort Wagner, the fortress that guarded the southern approach to Charleston Harbor.

As Pierce described events, the Fifty-fourth Regiment arrived at Morris Island, south of Charleston, about five o'clock on the afternoon of July 18. The men were worn and weary and hungry. Since the twelfth they had been involved in heavy fighting on nearby James Island, and had just spent two nights on the march in heavy thundershowers with little food. When his regiment arrived at Morris Island, Colonel Shaw sought out General Strong, his commanding general, and learned that if he wanted it, the chance to lead the assault on Fort Wagner in a few hours' time belonged to the Fifty-fourth Regiment. Swiftly looking over his six hundred exhausted troops, Shaw sized up his opportunity and said yes.

Charleston Harbor was well protected. The northern lip of its entrance was guarded by Forts Moultrie and Beauregard, both on Sullivan's Island. The southern lip boasted Fort Wagner and a smaller battery, Fort Gregg, both on Morris Island. In the center of the harbor, rising out of the sea, stood Fort Sumter, where the first shots of the Civil War had been fired. All these defenses were strongly occupied by the Confederates. It was the desire of General Quincy Gillmore, who had just replaced General Hunter as commander of the Department of the South, to wrest away from the rebels all these positions, beginning with Fort Wagner.

Wagner itself stretched across the neck of Morris Island near its northern end. It was known to be the strongest single earthwork in the country, a double barricade of turf and log revetment reinforced with sand, with a gorge protecting its southern face. All day on the eighteenth Union gunboats, monitors, and an ironsides had bombarded the fort, and it was thought by late in the day that most of the enemy had been driven out and the armament of Fort Wagner rendered harmless. Actually this was not the case. Wagner was well protected on the sea side by bombproofs, and instead of the few hundred rebels supposed to be left inside the fort, an actual seventeen hundred soldiers had withstood the bombardment and remained there. Against them the Fifty-fourth innocently was being sent, at the head of three brigades of Union infantry.

The men of the Fifty-fourth, six hundred strong, marched north along the ocean beach on Morris Island until they could see Fort Wagner in the distance. Its flag flew defiantly. In the gathering twilight the regiment paused on the sand to rest and await the signal to attack. Colonel Shaw walked calmly up and down the line. He wore a close-fitting staff officer's jacket, a silver eagle denoting his rank on each shoulder. His trousers were light blue. A narrow silk sash was wound around his waist beneath his jacket, and on his head he wore a high felt army hat with cord. From his sword belt hung his field officer's sword with his initials worked into the ornamentation of the guard. He looked composed and graceful, though his face was pale. To his friend Edward Pierce, whom he had encountered at General Strong's headquarters, Shaw had given his papers and letters, for he had a certain presentiment about the night ahead.

Suddenly a gray horse galloped down the beach, and General George Strong in full uniform, with yellow handkerchief bound around his neck, rode up with several aides and orderlies. He was there to address the men of the Fifty-fourth. Briefly he told them that they had been chosen to lead the assault because they were a strong regiment, well officered, and because he wanted to give them the chance they sought to prove their abilities.

"Boys, I am a Massachusetts man," he said loudly, "and I know you will fight for the honor of the state. I am sorry you must go into the fight tired and hungry, but the men in the fort are tired, too. There are but three hundred behind those walls, and they have been fighting all day. Don't fire a musket on the way up, but go in and bayonet them at their guns!"

The general called out the color-bearer. "If this man falls, who will lift the flag and carry it on?"

Colonel Shaw took a cigar from between his lips to say, "I will."

The men cheered loudly. General Strong shook hands with Colonel Shaw and rode off.

The next half hour seemed drawn out to eternity. Darkness was coming on rapidly, and there had been a partial resumption of the bombardment, so that every once in a while a cannonball fell somewhere nearby.

"I guess they kind of 'spec's we're coming," a soldier laughed nervously.

The officers moved about quietly, shaking hands with one another. They had tightened their sword belts and brought their revolvers around to the front. Finally, at 7:45 P.M., came the command.

"Attention!" shouted Colonel Shaw.

The regiment sprang to its feet.

"Move in quick time until within a hundred yards of the fort. Then double-quick and charge! Forward!"

The men moved rapidly up the beach, preserving

their formation well over the difficult ground. After a thousand yards the beach suddenly narrowed at a spot where a marsh projected itself toward the high-tide line. For want of room the men on the flanks were slowed and forced to fall behind while those in the center pressed on more freely. At that moment, while the Union soldiers were being squeezed in the defile, Fort Wagner opened fire. A stream of shot and shell came rattling and crashing among the Fifty-fourth, and a sheet of flame lit up the parapet of the fort. Men fell, but the great body of them changed to double-quick step and began running the last hundred yards into the steady fire. Officers with waving swords led charging men, and all raced through the alternating brightness and blackness toward the parapet. From the fort howitzers swept the advancing ranks, and musket fire rained down. The colored troops kept coming, climbing through the gorge half filled with water, and mounting the sloping wall beyond into the teeth of the enemy. Everywhere men fell, killed and wounded, but those at the head of the regiment gained the crest and fired for the first time down into the mass of upturned rebel faces. Reaching the rampart with the first of his men, Colonel Shaw shouted, "Forward, Fifty-fourth," and with uplifted sword took a bullet through his heart.

What followed was a nightmare. The Fifty-fourth was driven back from the parapet, and amidst the continuing havoc, those not dead or wounded formed a line in an artillery trench some seven hundred yards away and prepared to meet an expected counterattack.

Now in command of the regiment was the ninth captain in the line, for all officers preceding him in rank had been killed or wounded. While the black soldiers defended their line, the rest of General Strong's brigade, which had been slow in supporting the Fifty-fourth, moved into the attack. Behind them came the brigades of General Putnam. All met the same treatment the Fifty-fourth had received, although part of the Sixth Connecticut and Forty-eighth New York managed to push into the southeast bastion of the fort, where they were joined by survivors of three other regiments. These brave men kept a toehold in Fort Wagner for a devastating two hours, until they were forced to retreat with heavy casualties.

At 2:00 A.M. on the nineteenth of July the Fifty-fourth Massachusetts was relieved and sent to the rear. There the officers sadly counted their losses: three officers dead, including Colonel Shaw; eleven officers wounded, including Lieutenant Colonel Hallowell, who had received a ball in the groin. Among the enlisted men 256—over a third of the regiment—were dead, wounded, or missing and presumed captured. It was a heavy toll.

Not until the evening of July 20 did we at Port Royal hear the sickening news of the defeat. It seemed too terrible to believe, and for a while we kept up the vain hope that at least Colonel Shaw was somehow still alive, perhaps only wounded or captured. Then the wounded of the Fifty-fourth began to arrive in Beaufort, and we heard from their lips the truth: that Robert Gould Shaw had indeed fallen, and that his body, stripped of rank and clothing, was buried in a common trench with his soldiers at the foot of Fort Wagner's parapet. It was an unusual way to dispose of the body of an officer of Shaw's rank, and was undoubtedly intended as a gross insult by the Confederates. Yet, ironically, the rebels paid Shaw great honor, for it seemed particularly appropriate that he should share the grave of his troops. Hearing of a plan to recover the body, Shaw's father wrote to stop the action, saying he wished his son to lie where he had fallen. After the war the silk sash Robert Gould Shaw had worn about his waist on the last night of his life was sent to the Shaw family by the Confederate officer who had bought it as a trophy after the battle. And Shaw's sword, found resting on a Virginia mantelpiece, was likewise returned North. They were small recompense to the grieving widow and parents.

Among the soldiers of the Fifty-fourth, casualties were high. Fifty-four men were killed or died of battle wounds. One hundred forty-nine others were wounded but lived, while fifty-two men were missing and never accounted for. It was the twenty-nine Negroes who were captured, however, who drew the most attention and concern. When the two armies met to exchange prisoners under a flag of truce a few days later, the rebels refused to exchange their black captives. Action on the matter was swift. On the thirtieth of July President Lincoln issued a proclamation warning that if the enemy sold or enslaved any captured Union soldier, regardless of color, a rebel prisoner of war would be placed at hard labor. If the enemy put to death any

Union soldier, regardless of color, a rebel prisoner would be executed. This proclamation caused the Confederate army to stop reporting captured Negroes, which in turn led to a full year's suspension of prisoner exchanges. Only fifteen of the twenty-nine captured Negroes of the Fifty-fourth survived their prison experience, which was ghastly beyond words. Union prisoners suffered unbelievable treatment in the Southern jails and prison camps, and the black captives endured the worst treatment of all. Yet they were neither executed nor enslaved as had been threatened. Lincoln's proclamation was effective.

The remnant of the Fifty-fourth Regiment remained on Morris Island to participate in the eight-week siege that eventually overcame Forts Wagner and Sumter. But I was more concerned with that part of the regiment that straggled into the Beaufort hospital. For a week I went daily to help at the hospital, doing what I could by way of sewing up bullet holes and bayonet slashes in the pantaloons and jackets of the soldiers, helping to distribute medicines, talking a little with the men, and writing letters home for them. They were so brave. They complained little, though some of them had grievous wounds. Incredibly, or so it seemed to me, they responded to their hospitalization quite cheerfully. One young private badly wounded in the leg told me he counted himself lucky to be in a Union hospital, for had he been captured his leg would almost certainly have been amputated and his chances for survival drastically reduced.

While they lay convalescing, word came to the

wounded men that the black soldiers of the Fifty-
fourth would be paid only ten dollars a month for
their services instead of the promised thirteen. Dismay
and resentment and anger were in the men's voices as
they discussed this insulting news. Most of them swore
they would accept nothing less than their full wages,
and later I heard that the whole regiment refused to
take less than thirteen dollars a month. Eventually the
government paid the full amount. Meanwhile the
black soldiers went on fighting and dying like any
other Union troops, despite the threat of less recompense for laying down their lives.

By July's end I was sick at heart and sick in body as
well. The intense heat, the limited diet, and the exertions of teaching had taken their toll physically; the
defeat at Morris Island utterly vanquished my spirits.
My lungs felt weak, and I began to fear I would fall
victim to fever. Yet I would not have determined to
leave St. Helena had that course not been prescribed
by Dr. Rogers. He himself was ill and was returning
North for a few months' rest. Suddenly, on the last day
of July, I found myself joining him and Edward Pierce
and others from Port Royal aboard the *Fulton,* sailing
north from Hilton Head in the early morning. So swift
was my decision and my leavetaking that though I
packed a trunk, I was quickly separated from it, and it
arrived in Philadelphia many weeks after I did.

Steaming north from Port Royal, we passed at a distance Charleston Harbor and saw smoke from the
still-booming guns on Morris Island. We spoke sadly
of the beautiful, brave young colonel who had found a

grave there and of his heroic men—some dead beneath the walls, some prisoners and doomed to an unknown fate. We spoke of Colonel Higginson, who had gone North a week earlier, wounded on an ill-starred expedition the First South Carolina Volunteers had made up the South Edisto River to cut off the railroad at Jacksonboro, west of Charleston. We talked of young Ned Hallowell, also gone North to be nursed of his wounds at home in Philadelphia, who, when he recovered, would be the new colonel of the Fifty-fourth.

When, after two and a half calm beautiful days at sea, we steamed into New York Harbor, it seemed strange to be in a city, to see so many people, and odd that so many faces should be white! Next day I arrived home, taking everybody at Lombard Street by surprise. They swiftly rallied to the occasion by calling in friends and relatives to greet me and by mixing a batch of that wonderful, unspeakable new luxury which I tasted that day for the first time—ice cream!

Now ends my journal, though not, I hope, my usefulness. Who can speak to why we let our diary, which for many months or years has been our closest confidant, suddenly lie untouched? Perhaps we became too busy to put pen to paper. To record every experience is too time-consuming, while to record our distilled thoughts is too difficult. Or perhaps, and more likely, the heart goes out of us, and we need to start again another time, in some other life. So, I believe, it was with me, and this journal ends.

After a few weeks' rest I returned to St. Helena in October 1863 and went on teaching there for eight more months before going North again for good. While I was still in South Carolina that spring of 1864, I had good news from Father. He had been in London since the outbreak of the war, for he felt if free Negroes were not allowed to participate in the fight, he would do what he could in England to prevent Britain from coming to the aid of the Confederacy. When the situation at home changed and a call went out for Negro volunteers to join the army, Father tied up his business affairs in London and came home. In the early spring of 1864, at the age of fifty, he enlisted as a private in the Forty-third United States Colored Infantry. He was promptly made sergeant major and, since he was too old for active duty, he was assigned to recruiting service in Maryland. In his new capacity he made many effective speeches encouraging his fellow black men to enlist and bring prompt end to civil war.

Then suddenly, in late April, Father contracted erysipelas and within a few days was dead. I can scarcely tell you of the shock to me. I, who had not seen Father for three full years, would now never see him. By the time word came to me at Port Royal his funeral was over, and I must take what solace I could from reading his obituary notices.

His was no ordinary funeral, and perhaps there was comfort in that. For the first time in America a Negro —my father, Robert Bridges Forten—was buried with full military honors. There was a service at our home on Lombard Street, where J. Miller McKim and Lucretia Mott and others spoke appropriately to a small group of family and friends. Then Father's coffin was carried through the streets of Philadelphia to the African Episcopal Church of St. Thomas by sixteen uniformed comrades of the Forty-third Regiment. A large escort of officers, soldiers, and citizens followed behind to hear the last rites said and to witness three volleys fired over his grave.

Perhaps Father's death is fit conclusion to my tale, which began with a black fugitive in chains and ends, just ten years later, with a Negro accorded a ceremony of free men. How long it takes to move the minds and spirits of mankind a degree! Yet as has been said often enough, the longest journey begins with a step, and though I cannot see far into the future, I only pray it does not end there as well.

Farewell.

Epilogue

~·~·~·~·~·~·~·~·~·~·~·~·~·~·~·~·~·~·~·

One word more.

If I were to write a novel about slavery, that melodrama I have always been tempted to write, I might invent a plot like this:

Once upon a time two daughters of an old, aristocratic Southern family were led by their consciences to rebel against the tradition in which they were raised. Their names were Sarah and Angelina Grimké. They were the children of John Grimké, a judge of the state of South Carolina and a man of wealth, social position, and political prominence.

Sarah and Angelina and their nine brothers and sisters grew up in Charleston, South Carolina, in a home staffed by Negro slaves. Half of the year they spent on their Beaufort rice and cotton plantation, where slaves labored in the fields and performed the chores that permitted the Grimkés to live in comfort.

Having been born into a slaveholding family, and having since childhood been dressed and fed by black hands, having witnessed and found abhorrent the darker side of slavery, in which Negro servants were cruelly punished by the "gentlewomen" who owned them, in which field hands were tortured for misdemeanors, in which mulatto children were born into slavery, in which black humans were sold away from their families at their master's convenience, in which slaves were kept abysmally ignorant, having seen and known all these things, the two Southern sisters left home and went to live in the North.

For a time Sarah and Angelina found peace within the Quaker movement in Philadelphia. But turning their backs upon slavery was not enough. The consciences of the Grimké sisters spoke louder. They soon joined the newly formed Philadelphia Female Anti-Slavery Society and began listening to antislavery lecturers and reading antislavery publications. Angelina was moved to write a letter of admiration to the fiery editor of the new Boston publication, the *Liberator*. Garrison published her letter without asking the author's permission. In so doing he pushed Angelina Grimké into the limelight, a place no woman, especially not one who was a Quaker, should be. The year was 1835. Women did not speak out in public, nor did they offer opinions on controversial subjects, nor openly espouse unpopular causes. The Philadelphia

Society of Friends rebuked both Grimké sisters in numerous ways.

Still following their consciences, which dictated that freedom and equality should be enjoyed by all men, black or white, the sisters left the Quakers and daringly agreed to become the first women agents of the American Anti-Slavery Society. In that capacity they would give "parlor talks" to small groups of women in private homes.

But no parlor was large enough to hold the crowds of women who wanted to hear Sarah and Angelina Grimké describe from their experience conditions among the slaves. The sisters found themselves standing in churches and schools, addressing audiences that contained men as well as women. Modest as they were personally, and straightforward and unsensational as their talks were, the Grimkés very shortly became notorious. Newspapers across the nation ridiculed these two females who "flaunted themselves in public" to champion abolition, who pointed accusing fingers at Northern prejudice, who criticized the incriminating silence of Northern churches and the exploitive acts of Northern merchants and bankers.

The Congregational ministers of Massachusetts issued a pastoral letter amounting to a tirade against Angelina and Sarah Grimké and their efforts at reform. But the sisters continued to travel about New England, lecturing. They also took up their pens. Angelina wrote an *Appeal to the Christian Women of the South,* urging Southern women to exert every influence to rid the country of slavery. For her pains she was cursed in the South and threatened with imprisonment should she ever return to Charleston. Sarah wrote an *Epistle to the Clergy of the Southern States* that was scarcely less popular. Going a step further, the sisters demonstrated their beliefs by persuading their mother to give them their share of the family slaves, and then freeing those slaves.

Sarah and Angelina were chewing another bone of contention along with slavery. They had received, as they grew up, an education considered appropriate for wealthy young ladies of Charleston. It was well grounded in embroidery and deportment and the social graces, with enough reading, writing, arithmetic, and French thrown in to give the suggestion of culture. But the Grimké sons had studied history and geography and Latin, and had gone to Northern universities and had studied law and medicine and religion! Growing up, Sarah smoldered with resentment at the differences in treatment based upon sex. She longed to study Latin, but her father forbade it. She wanted to be a lawyer, but her brothers hooted. The minds of women, it was assumed, were not strong enough for such things.

Sarah objected, too, to the way Southern men placed their "delicate" wives and sisters on pedestals while they made concubines of their slaves and raised mulatto slave children in their own households. Her indignation at this double standard finally found expression in a pamphlet called *Letters on the Equality of the Sexes and the Condition of Women.*

Antislavery and women's rights, the two causes gained strength in tandem as the influence of the Grimké sisters grew. Symbolic of the progress in both areas was an address made in 1838 by Angelina before the Massachusetts legislature on the subject of slavery. It was the first time a woman had ever spoken before that body, and she was warmly received.

Picking up another thread of my story, I would next introduce my readers to a gentleman whose career was even more remarkable than the Grimkés'. His name was Theodore Dwight Weld, and he was a Congregational minister who descended from several lines of distinguished New England Puritans—the Dwights, the Edwards, and the Hutchinsons.

Theodore Weld was an abolitionist, and he had a powerful gift for oratory. He was tall and thin, unkempt-looking, with dark, brooding features and sonorous voice. He possessed great physical energy as well as enormous personal charm, and when he spoke, his gloomy face was transfigured by sincerity and kindliness. These qualities, together with keen intellect and a golden tongue, made Weld one of the most effective antislavery orators ever to mount the abolition platform.

During the early 1830's Weld carried the abolition crusade to Western Reserve College in Ohio, there indoctrinating the entire faculty with his beliefs. He went on to Ohio's Lane Seminary, where the famous preacher Lyman Beecher was president, and established an abolition society among the students. But when he organized a series of debates among the Lane students on the topic of immediate emancipation, Weld sundered the university. "Logic on fire," Beecher called Weld as four fifths of the students, most of them mature men in their late twenties, left Lane Seminary in dissent against the antiabolitionist administrators of the institution.

Some of the Lane students went to Oberlin, Ohio, to help found Oberlin College. Others became members of Weld's antislavery crusade, spreading throughout New York, Pennsylvania, and Ohio as apostles of abolition. Night after night in town after town they spoke against slavery. It was hard work, ill-rewarded, for the opinions of these antislavery missionaries were not everywhere popular. Weld was frequently booed and hissed, and occasionally he was mobbed or struck by stones, eggs, and vegetables. In addition, he must travel in all kinds of weather, eat inadequate meals, sleep in poor accommodations, or do without sleep entirely. Despite such trials, his powerful voice spoke on. An admirer claimed that one hour of Weld's oratory could persuade a liquor merchant to empty his vats. But the strenuous pace of these activities eventually took its toll. Within a few years Weld's health was seriously impaired, and his vocal cords could produce sounds only slightly louder than a whisper. He had to stop traveling and speaking for antislavery.

For a time Theodore Weld helped Garrison publish the *Liberator* in Boston. Then he gravitated to the New York offices of the American Anti-Slavery Society. At that society's annual convention in 1837

Weld met the Grimké sisters, and a year later he married Angelina.

In a sense Weld married the Grimké sisters, for Sarah always lived with Theodore and Angelina and shared in their ventures and helped raise their children. One of the first things this remarkable trio did was to produce the most powerful antislavery tract that had ever been written or would be written until *Uncle Tom's Cabin* appeared. By scanning the back issues of hundreds of Southern newspapers, by assembling testimony from every manner of slaveholder and slave dealer, and by poring over judicial decisions and law codes, they brought together in one volume documented evidence of all the horrible aspects of slavery. The book was called *American Slavery As It Is*. It was published in 1839 and sold over a hundred thousand copies in its first year of publication. I have earlier mentioned the overpowering impression it made upon me when I read it as a child.

Another of their ventures was a school, which Theodore, Angelina, and Sarah organized in northern New Jersey. Eagleswood was originally part of an experiment in cooperative living of the Raritan Bay Colony. Though the experiment eventually fell apart, Weld's school was so successful that it continued independently. Eagleswood was a boarding school which tried out many then daring ideas. It was coeducational, and it was interracial. It had a rich curriculum that ranged from classical subjects to manual arts and agriculture and housekeeping, and included art and music and

even gymnastic exercises for women. The young ladies, including the Grimké sisters themselves, clad in
bloomer costume and swinging Indian clubs, inspired
some sensational comment.

Theodore Weld believed that school and real life
should be an integrated whole. He took his scholars on
expeditions to neighboring towns and into the city,
and invited interesting people to come to Eagleswood
to talk. Thoreau, Emerson, Horace Greeley, and a
long list of people representing many beliefs and many
reforms came to Eagleswood and enjoyed the atmosphere of free inquiry they found there.

One winter evening soon after the Civil War, Angelina was reading a copy of the *Anti-Slavery Standard*
when she came across the name Grimké in a surprising
context. Her family name, she knew, was limited to
her immediate relatives who had lived in Charleston.
Her brothers had all grown to become men of affairs.
Henry had become a successful lawyer, planter, and
slaveholder, but was now dead. John, a highly respected Charleston doctor, was also dead, and so was
Charles. Frederick was a judge in Ohio. He had written an important book called *The Nature and Ten-
dency of Free Institutions,* and though he was strongly
opposed to organized abolition, he and Sarah corresponded regularly about their conflicting points of
view.

Thomas was the brother with whom Angelina and
Sarah had been closest during his life. He had first
studied for the ministry, but then turned to law instead and became prominent in South Carolina poli-

tics. He wrestled with his conscience over the problem
of slavery, and though he could not rid himself of his
innate Southern belief in the inferiority of the slave,
he worked hard to strengthen the American Colonization Society in South Carolina, the most effective solution he saw to the problem. Thomas was also a strong
Union man and as state senator was influential in
patching some of the early cracks that appeared in
North-South relations. In fact, Angelina and Sarah
were even feeling hopeful of bringing Thomas to see
their own antislavery views, when he died and they
were left with only his papers to edit.

But Angelina knew that the Mr. Grimké mentioned
in the *Anti-Slavery Standard* as having delivered a fine
address at Lincoln University, a colored institution in
Pennsylvania, could not be her only surviving brother,
Frederick. Perhaps it was a former Grimké slave who
had taken the family name. Angelina wrote "Mr.
Grimké" to find out who he was, and his prompt answer amazed her.

Archibald Grimké's reply introduced himself as Angelina's nephew. He was the Negro son born of her
brother Henry and one of his slaves, Nancy Weston,
whom Henry Grimké had lived with after the death of
his wife.

Archibald sketched his own life and that of his two
brothers, who were also sons of Henry Grimké. When
Henry Grimké died, his three colored offspring—
Francis, Archibald, and John—were left under the
guardianship of their white halfbrother, Montague. At
the outbreak of the Civil War, Montague decided to

sell the three boys. Archibald ran away. Francis did, too, but he was found and sold into slavery along with John. After the war the three were reunited and free in Charleston. Agents of the United States Sanitary Commission working in Charleston were impressed by the obvious intelligence of Francis and Archibald and sent them to Boston to go to school. In 1866 the two young men, aged sixteen and seventeen, entered Lincoln University, where they were excellent students. In the course of pursuing his studies, Archibald Grimké's name had been mentioned in print and Angelina had seen it.

What was the reaction of Sarah and Angelina on learning of the existence of their black nephews? Angelina wrote them acknowledging the relationship and charging them to bear proudly the once honored name of Grimké. In letters that followed, both Sarah and Angelina proffered their interest and concern for the welfare of Archibald and Francis. They also contributed to the boys' expenses despite the extremely modest Weld income. When the young men graduated from Lincoln University, Angelina and her son attended the commencement exercises. Francis was valedictorian of his class, and Archibald ranked third.

The two young black men visited the Weld home and before long came to consider it their own. The Welds and Sarah Grimké, in turn, considered Archibald and Francis part of the family, and devoted time and attention to charting their future.

Archibald decided to become a lawyer. He stayed at Lincoln to earn his master's degree, then attended and graduated with distinction from Harvard Law School. An LL.B. in his hand, he stayed on in Boston, where his law practice thrived. For twelve years he published the leading Negro newspaper in the city and was an outstanding leader of his race. In 1894 Archibald became United States Consul to the Republic of Santo Domingo for four years. He later became president of the American Negro Academy in Washington, and during his busy lifetime wrote several books, including fine biographies of William Lloyd Garrison and Charles Sumner.

Francis Grimké also studied law for a time, but in 1875 decided instead to enter Princeton Theological Seminary. For most of the rest of his long life he served as minister of the Fifteenth Street Presbyterian Church in Washington, D. C. There he ministered with distinction to the Negro people of his parish and of the whole nation, fighting for Negro rights through his sermons and his writings. He was assisted in his life's work by his wife, Charlotte Forten Grimké.

And now you have learned, if you did not know already, that this is no mere fiction I have been tracing. Francis Grimké and I were married in 1878, shortly before he graduated from Princeton Seminary. For me, finding Frank was the end of long years of great inner loneliness. Friends and acquaintances had always been mine in abundance, yet never before had I known real intimacy with another human being. While I had been accepted and respected by many fine white men and women who were genuinely intolerant of prejudice, yet there was always the fine line of difference between us. And while I liked and admired many people of my own race in the North and in the South, yet there was none outside the Forten and Purvis families whose experiences had been enough like mine to draw us close. The bond between me and other blacks, freedmen and slaves, came from our common yearning to improve the welfare of our race and to reestablish ourselves as capable human beings after the chattel years.

In Francis Grimké, however, I found an intimate friend, and though he is several years younger than I, we love one another with that joy and satisfaction that comes of finding fulfillment in another human creature. Together we have led long and happy and useful lives. Our one child, a daughter, died soon after she was born, and this sorrow has been the greatest we have borne. Rather than dwell upon it, I wish instead I could tell you of our years of struggle, triumph, and defeat in helping our race in the throes of its turmoil adjusting to freedom after the Civil War. The story of the fight for political and civil and social rights for the Negro, the tale of how my people gained toeholds in legislatures in their states, only to be foully and rudely pushed down, makes exceedingly dark history. So does the less well-documented tale of that insidious influence, prejudice, which makes men evil and inhumane toward other men. All this cannot be contained here and must wait for another volume.

Although Sarah Grimké died before I could know her personally, and though I knew Angelina Grimké Weld only as a paralyzed invalid the last two years of her life, I did know and love Theodore Weld. He was a grand old man, tall, with his brilliant face shining out from a great mass of white hair and beard. He once told me how proud Angelina and Sarah had been of the accomplishments of Archibald and Francis Grimké. It was a wonderful irony, said Weld, that the Negro Grimkés should have carried on the family name in triumph, for none of Sarah and Angelina's other nephews amounted to anything special.

And now, indeed, farewell.

Bibliography

~~~~~~

BACKGROUND READING

* BARNES, GILBERT HOBBS. *The Anti-Slavery Impulse, 1830–1844.* Third edition, New York, 1964.

BILLINGTON, R. A. "James Forten, Forgotten Abolitionist," *Negro History Bulletin.* November 1949.

BUCKMASTER, HENRIETTA. *Let My People Go: The Story of the Underground Railroad and the Growth of the Abolition Movement.* New York, 1941.

* CASH, W. J. *The Mind of the South.* New York, 1941.

* COMMAGER, HENRY STEELE. *Theodore Parker: Yankee Crusader.* Boston, 1936.

DOUTY, ESTHER M. *Forten the Sailmaker.* Chicago, 1968.

* Available in paperback

234

* ELKINS, STANLEY M. *Slavery: A Problem in American Institutional & Intellectual Life.* Chicago, 1959.

* FILLER, LOUIS. *The Crusade Against Slavery, 1830–1860.* New York, 1960.

* FISHER, MILES MARK. *Negro Slave Songs in the United States.* Second edition, New York, 1963.

FRANKLIN, JOHN HOPE. *From Slavery to Freedom.* New York, 1947.

JOHNSON, GUION G. *A Social History of the Sea Islands with Special Reference to St. Helena Island, South Carolina.* Chapel Hill, 1930.

Journal of Negro History. Washington, 1917–1969. Its volumes contain many pertinent articles.

LERNER, GERDA. *The Grimké Sisters From South Carolina.* Boston, 1967.

MERRILL, WALTER M. *Against Wind and Tide: A Biography of William Lloyd Garrison.* Boston, 1963.

MEYER, HOWARD N. *Colonel of the Black Regiment: The Life of Thomas Wentworth Higginson.* New York, 1967.

Negro History Bulletin. Washington, 1937–1969. Its volumes contain many pertinent articles.

THARP, LOUISE HALL. *The Peabody Sisters of Salem.* Boston, 1950.

TURNER, EDWARD RAYMOND. *The Negro in Pennsylvania: Slavery, Servitude, Freedom, 1839–1861.* Washington, 1911.

WELLS, ANNA MARY. *Dear Preceptor, the Life and Times of Thomas Wentworth Higginson.* Boston, 1963.

WOODSON, CARTER G. *The Negro in Our History.* Washington, 1941.

CONTEMPORARY MATERIALS

* APTHEKER, HERBERT, ed. *A Documentary History of the Negro People in the United States.* New York, 1951.

———. *One Continual Cry: David Walker's Appeal to the Colored Citizens of the World, 1829–1830; Its Meaning: 1965.* New York, 1965.

* BILLINGTON, R. A., ed. *A Free Negro in the Slave Era: The Journal of Charlotte L. Forten.* Paperback edition, New York, 1961.

BROWN, WILLIAM W. *Narrative of William W. Brown, A Fugitive Slave.* Boston, 1847.

———. *The Black Man: His Antecedents, His Genius and His Achievements.* New York, 1863.

CHILD, LYDIA MARIA. *An Appeal in Favor of that Class of Americans Called Africans.* Boston, 1833.

* DOUGLASS, FREDERICK. *My Bondage and My Freedom.* New York, 1855.

———. *Narrative of the Life of Frederick Douglass.* Boston, 1845. Paperback edition, Boston, 1960.

EMILIO, LUIS F. *History of the Fifty-Fourth Regiment of Massachusetts Volunteer Infantry.* Boston, 1891.

FORTEN, CHARLOTTE. "Life on the Sea Islands," *Atlantic Monthly.* May 1864, June 1864.

* HIGGINSON, THOMAS WENTWORTH. *Army Life in a Black Regiment.* Paperback edition, New York, 1962.

———. *Cheerful Yesterdays.* Boston, 1909.

———. *Contemporaries.* Boston, 1899.

HOLLAND, RUPERT S., ed. *Letters and Diary of Laura M. Towne Written From the Sea Islands of South Carolina, 1862–1884.* Cambridge, 1912.

KEMBLE, FANNY. *Journal of a Residence on a Georgia Plantation in 1838–39.* New York, 1863.

The Liberator. Boston, 1831–1865.

The National Anti-Slavery Standard. New York, 1840–1872.

PEARSON, ELIZABETH W., ed. *Letters From Port Royal Written at the Time of the Civil War.* Nodyon, 1906.

PIERCE, EDWARD L. "The Freedmen At Port Royal," *Atlantic Monthly.* September 1863.

STILL, WILLIAM. *The Underground Railroad: A Record of Facts, Authentic Narratives, Letters, etc.* Philadelphia, 1879.

WELD, THEODORE. *American Slavery As It Is.* New York, 1839.

WILSON, DAVID, ed. *Narrative of Solomon Northup.* Buffalo, 1853.

Index

~~~~~~

About the Author

Polly Ormsby Longsworth grew up in Waterford, New York. She was graduated from Emma Willard School and Smith College. She and her four children live in Amherst, Massachusetts, where her husband is vice-president of Hampshire College.

When she undertook the story of Charlotte Forten, Mrs. Longsworth had recently completed *Emily Dickinson: Her Letter to the World*. She was fascinated by the vast differences in the lives of the poet and the free Negro girl, who were New England contemporaries for a time. While Emily read about the struggles of the abolitionists, knew of the vast surge of humanitarian reform, and corresponded regularly with reformer Thomas Wentworth Higginson about literary matters, these affairs of the world were outside her concern. Charlotte, on the other hand, was completely caught up in them.

Writing about the nineteenth century at the same time so much turmoil concerning civil rights and black nationalism was occurring in the twentieth century was an absorbing experience for the author. It provided many unusual insights, ironies, and parallels to the ongoing struggle for equal opportunity for the black American.